The Association of
Accountants and
Financial Professionals
in Business

T0087533

Curt Verschoor On Ethics
Timely Columns from *Strategic Finance* Magazine

Curt Verschoor

Edited by Belverd E. Needles, Jr.

About IMA®

IMA (Institute of Management Accountants) is one of the largest and most respected associations focused exclusively on advancing the management accounting profession. Globally, IMA supports the profession through research, the CMA® (Certified Management Accountant) program, CSCA® (Certified in Strategy and Competitive Analysis) credential, continuing education, networking, and advocacy of the highest ethical business practices. To learn more about IMA's ethics resources, visit IMA's Ethics Center: www.imanet.org/ethicscenter.

About the CMA®

IMA's globally recognized CMA (Certified Management Accountant) is the leading certification for management accountants and financial professionals in business. Earning the CMA requires a mastery of advanced-level knowledge in four critical areas: financial planning, analysis, control, and decision support. For more information about the CMA certification program, please visit www.imanet.org/certification.

ISBN: 978-0-9967293-9-0 (paper)
ISBN: 978-1-119-72215-1 (ePub)
ISBN: 978-1-119-72212-0 (ePDF)

V10019307_062320

Table of Contents

Table of Contents

ABOUT THE AUTHOR: CURTIS C. VERSCHOOR, CMA, CPA, CIA, CFE

Curtis C. Verschoor, CMA, CPA, CIA, CFE, Ed.D. in Business, Northern Illinois University; MBA and BBA, University of Michigan at Ann Arbor. Former Corporate Controller of the Colgate-Palmolive Company and Baxter International, CFO of a diversified public corporation, and former Chief Internal Audit Executive of The Singer Company. Former National Director of Education at Touche Ross & Co., predecessor of Deloitte.

Verschoor consults and is a prolific author on business and professional ethics, and serves as an expert witness on auditing subjects. He serves on the board of directors and audit committees of nonprofit organizations and is a contributing editor for several academic and practitioner journals.

He is currently Emeritus Ledger & Quill Research Professor in the School of Accountancy and Management Information Systems and Honorary Senior Wicklander Research Fellow in the Institute for Business and Professional Ethics, both at DePaul University; a Research Scholar in the Center for Business Ethics at Bentley University; former Fellow of the Corporate Governance Center at Kennesaw State University; and former Honorary Visiting Professor in the Centre for Research in Corporate Governance at the Sir John Cass Business School In London.

Verschoor has served several professional organizations including membership on senior global technical committees of the American Institute of Certified Public Accountants (AICPA), Financial Executives International (FEI), and the Institute of Internal Auditors (IIA) and is current Chair-Emeritus of the Ethics Committee of IMA® (Institute of Management Accountants).

In 2016, Verschoor was awarded a Lifetime Achievement Award by Trust Across America – Trust Around the World as a top thought leader in trustworthy business.

He can be reached at curtisverschoor@sbcglobal.net.

Belverd E. Needles, Jr., Ph.D., CMA, CPA, EY Distinguished Professor of Accounting. Driehaus College of Business School of Accountancy, DePaul University (USA). He is an internationally recognized expert in international financial reporting and auditing. He teaches financial accounting and auditing at DePaul University and has many years' experience in executive education. His textbooks, including *Principles of Accounting* (12th ed.), *Financial Accounting* (11th ed.), and *International Financial Reporting Standards: An Introduction* (3rd ed.) are used throughout the world. He has published in leading journals, including most recently on the subject of strategy, financial, and sustainability characteristics of high-performance companies.

Active in many academic and professional organizations, he was president of the International Association for Accounting Education and Research (IAAER) from 1997-2002 and currently serves as Vice-Chair of the Board of Advisors. He served as Vice President-Education of the American Accounting Association (2010-2011) and served on the Consultative Group on International Financial Reporting Standards to the United Nations. He is past Chair of the Board of Directors of the Illinois CPA Society and past president of the IAAER. He served as the elected U.S. representative to the European Accounting Association and president of the Federation of Schools of Accountancy. He served on the Consultative Group of the forerunner to the International Accounting Standards Board (IASB) and on the Education Committee of the International Federation of Accountants (IFAC). He served 15 years on the Board of Directors and as Chair of the Audit Committee of Ziegler Companies, Inc., a capital markets and financial services company.

He has received the Distinguished Alumni Award from Texas Tech University, the Illinois CPA Society Outstanding Educator Award and its Lifetime Achievement Award, and the Joseph A. Silvoso Faculty Award of Merit from the Federation of Schools of Accountancy. He was named Educator of the Year by the American Institute of CPAs, Accountant of the Year for Education by the national honorary society Beta Alpha Psi, and Outstanding International Accounting Educator as well as Lifetime Achievement in Service to Accounting Education by the American Accounting Association.

DePaul University awarded him the Wicklander Fellowship in Business Ethics, the Ledger & Quill Award of Merit, and the Ledger & Quill Teaching Excellence Award.

He received BBA and MBA degrees from Texas Tech University and the Ph.D. from the University of Illinois at Urbana/Champaign.

Introduction

For companies, professional organizations, and individuals to survive and grow over the long term, they must commit to aligning their plans, people, and activities to ethical behavior. We all know of examples where some have benefited in the short term by unethical behavior—the Enrons, Volkswagens, and Bernie Madoffs of the world, but eventually the house of cards crumbles. This proposition is the theme of the book *Driven* by Mark L. Frigo and Joel Litman.

Dr. Curtis C. Verschoor demonstrated years ago that a strong ethics policy does indeed help a firm increase its profits, but only if the policy is effectively monitored and enforced over the long run and embedded in the culture of the organization. His research has been published in top academic and professional journals.

In short, a company's attitudes in dealing with customers, employees, and social issues almost inevitably become known to the public, and then affect the company's sales and the profits of its shareholders.

"Having an effective code of ethics should become an icon of a well-run company," Verschoor said. "There is a great synergy between doing well with your customers and your employees and doing well by your shareholders. But we can't just look for what companies say. We have to look at what companies do."

Verschoor's study found that more than 75% of consumers claim they would switch brands to support companies dealing more favorably with these issues. Corporate culture is decisive in determining whether an organization will do the right thing, according to a recent report by the ACCA.

A member of IMA® (Institute of Management Accountants) for more than 40 years, Verschoor helped to revitalize the IMA Committee on Ethics, serving as a member for more than 20 years and Chair from 2014 to 2016. His research linking an ethical commitment to superior financial performance led to his interest beginning in 1999

in editing and writing a monthly column in *Strategic Finance,* the award-winning monthly magazine of IMA.

Since that time, Verschoor has advocated high ethical behavior in business through his monthly columns, which have received the highest marks in readership surveys. For more than 215 consecutive months, these columns have appeared in this professional magazine. Each essay is interesting, instructive, and stimulating.

This volume attempts what might be considered the impossible: to select and organize the best of these ethics essays. Our goal is to choose those essays that are of lasting value; essays that we can all learn from, whether you are a CMA® (Certified Management Accountant), Certified Public Accountant (CPA), or both and whether you work in industry, public accounting, government, or another field that uses your accounting knowledge and expertise, you are expected to maintain a high level of professional ethics. Verschoor's columns selected for this book are arranged by topic to facilitate the user's objectives and cover a wide variety of subject areas and include case studies, descriptions of landmark ethical developments, ethics advocacy, and others. It is envisioned that this book may be used in a number of ways. It serves as a resource for the business and/or accounting and finance professional to learn and reinforce ethical behavior both in themselves and in their organizations. In an organization setting, the columns can also function as the basis for discussion in professional education programs.

In academia, the columns can serve as assigned readings covering significant ethics events and issues, supporting a course in financial

Introduction

accounting or auditing. By assigning the readings as background for the topics they are teaching, faculty provide students with a foundation of support for ethical behavior. The columns can also be useful as the source for assigned papers or classroom discussion. IMA chapters and councils may also use the columns for continuing ethics education programs.

The Table of Contents contains a brief summary of each column that is classified into one of 12 chapters with the following topic areas:

Value of a Strong Ethical Culture

Studies of Ethical and Unethical Culture

Public and Management Accounting Ethics

Ethics of Executive Compensation

International Ethics Standards

Fraud Case Studies

Small Organization Fraud Studies

Regulation and Enforcement

Whistleblowing

Sustainability and Integrated Reporting

Tax Avoidance Issues

Students

The Value of an Ethical Corporate Culture

An independent U.S. research study conducted by LRN, a provider of governance, ethics, and compliance management, shows additional evidence that a company's ability to maintain an ethical corporate culture is key to the attraction, retention, and productivity of employees. In other words, money invested in ethics education, help lines, assessment of ethics programs, and risk evaluation is money well spent. *The LRN Ethics Study* involved 834 full-time employees from various industries across the United States. Respondents included both men and women, all 18 or older.

According to the LRN study, 94% of employees said it is either critical or important that the company they work for is ethical. This compares to 76% who said so in a similar survey six months earlier. Eighty-two percent said they would rather be paid less but work at a company that had ethical business practices than receive higher pay at a company with questionable ethics. More than a third (36%) had left a job because they disagreed with the actions of either fellow employees or managers. This is true across all ages, genders, and socioeconomic factors.

Other findings of the survey include 80% of respondents reporting that a disagreement with the ethics of a supervisor, fellow employee, or management was the most important reason for leaving a job and 21% citing pressure to engage in illegal activity.

Working for an ethical company is slightly more critical to women (63%) than to men (53%). Full-time employees in the western and southern U.S. consider the factor more important than those in the north central and northeast. Two-thirds of those in managerial and professional occupations find ethics important, compared to 45% of blue-collar workers.

The LRN study found that a majority (56%) of Americans working full-time say their current employer embraces ethics and corporate values in everything they do. Despite this, about 25% have witnessed unethical or even illegal behavior at their job in the past six months. Among those, only 11% say they weren't affected by it. About 30%

of respondents say their company merely toes the line by following the letter of the law and company policy. Nine percent say they work at a company where they either do what they are told and aren't encouraged to ask questions about what is right or wrong or they often see management and peers acting in questionable ways.

Among those who witness unethical behavior, about one in four say they do so at least once a week, including 12% who say it is a daily occurrence. Unethical behavior affects a company's costs and ability to recruit, train, and retain employees; increases the legal, regulatory, and compliance risks a company faces; and has an impact on productivity. Half of all respondents indicated that unethical behavior was a distraction on the job. While most merely spent time discussing ethical issues with colleagues, nearly one-third (32%) made a formal complaint or went to speak with management about a specific issue.

Dov Seidman, chairman and CEO of LRN, believes, "An ethical culture where employees and management use values and not rules to self-govern can only take root when executives, managers, supervisors, and employees understand and embrace the company's principles and values and incorporate them into their daily conduct."

George S. May International Company, a consulting firm that specializes in helping small and midsize businesses, has developed the three "Rs" of business ethics: respect, responsibility, and results.

Respect includes behavior such as:

*   Treating everyone (customers, coworkers, vendors, etc.) with dignity and courtesy.

*   Using company supplies, equipment, time, and money appropriately, efficiently, and for business purposes only.

*   Protecting and improving your work environment and abiding by laws, rules, and regulations that exist to protect our world and our way of life.

Responsibility applies to customers, coworkers, the organization, and yourself. Included are behaviors such as:

*   Providing timely, high-quality goods and services.

*   Working collaboratively and carrying your share of the load.

*   Meeting all performance expectations and adding value.

Essential for attaining results is an understanding that the way they are attained—the "means"—are every bit as and maybe more important than the ultimate goal—the "ends." The phrase "the ends justify the means" is an excuse that is used too often to explain an emotional response or action that wasn't well planned or considered carefully.

The May firm suggests that considering the three "Rs" before taking action will help you avoid the following common rationalizations:

*   Everyone else does it.

*   They'll never miss it.

*   Nobody will care.

*   The boss does it.

*   No one will know.

*   I don't have time to do it right.

*   That's close enough.

*   Some rules were meant to be broken.

*   It's not my job.

Is Business Ethics Getting Better or Worse?

Several recently published reports discussing the incidence of fraud within the business environment provide conflicting evidence as to whether the rate of wrongdoing in companies is increasing or decreasing. It's possible that the rate for some kinds of misdeeds might be decreasing in the United States but growing globally.

One report that describes increasing unethical behavior is the *2014 Global Economic Crime Survey* (GECS), "Economic Crime: A Threat to Business Globally," published by PricewaterhouseCoopers (PwC). This report says that global economic crime continues to be a major concern for organizations of all sizes, across all regions, and in virtually every sector, as 37% of all organizations report being hit by economic crime. Fraud rates increased from 30% of companies in 2009 to 34% in 2011 and 37% in 2014.

According to the survey, the five most common types of fraud consistently reported are asset misappropriation (69%), procurement fraud (29%), bribery and corruption (27%), cybercrime (24%), and accounting fraud (22%). The highest levels of economic crime are consistently reported by respondents in Africa (50%) and North America (41%), and the lowest levels are reported in the Middle East (21%). According to PwC's Steven Skalak, "The real story is that economic crime is threatening your business processes, eroding the integrity of your employees, and tarnishing your reputation."

The U.S. Supplement to the survey (GECS-U.S.) reports that 45% of responding U.S. organizations suffered from economic crime in the past two years, and 71% of respondents perceived an increased risk within that period. The study states, "54% of U.S. respondents reported their companies experienced fraud in excess of $100,000 with 8% reporting fraud in excess of $5 million." Asset misappropriation continues to be the largest type of misdoing, but it has dropped in significance from 93% in 2011 to 69% in 2014.

Cybercrime was the second-largest crime category at 44%, a slight increase from 40% in 2011. Accounting fraud increased from 16% in 2011 to 23% in 2014. Procurement fraud was introduced to the

study in 2014 and is the third-largest fraud category, amounting to an incidence rate of 27%. The major aspects of procurement fraud occur at the vendor level, where key participants in the process influence vendor selection or maintenance. Procurement fraud during the payment process occurred in 43% of the cases, both in the U.S. and globally.

The U.S. General Services Administration (GSA) Office of Inspector General describes some of the mechanisms:

- **Bid Rigging.** Fraud that impedes free and open competitive bidding to obtain the best goods and services at the lowest price.

- **Kickbacks.** Any money, fee, commission, gift, credit, gratuity, or item of value that is provided either directly or indirectly in exchange for preferential treatment.

- **Bribery.** The offering, receiving/giving, or soliciting of anything of value to influence action as an official or in discharge of legal or public duty.

- **Collusion.** The secret combination, conspiracy, or concert of action between two or more persons for fraudulent or deceitful purpose.

The GECS-U.S. also reports that bribery and corruption are on the rise and present a higher risk than money laundering and anticompetitive practices. Although only 14% of global and U.S. companies reported their organization had been asked to pay a bribe in the last 24 months, the risk of bribery and corruption is growing as companies increasingly operate and pursue opportunities in high-risk markets. As sales and marketing staffs experience pressure to deliver higher sales, the risk of bribery and corruption is likely to increase.

Is Business Ethics Getting Better or Worse?

More favorable news is provided by the 2013 *National Business Ethics Survey®* (NBES), published by the Ethics Resource Center (ERC). This survey is frequently described as the national benchmark for business ethics, and the ERC is devoted to independent research and the advancement of high ethical standards and practices in public and private organizations.

The report found that the amount of misconduct in U.S. businesses declined substantially for the third straight survey, putting it at the lowest point since the ERC began conducting the survey. There was other positive news as well. The percentage of workers who observed misconduct dipped from 45% in 2011 to 41% in 2013, yet this is still a large proportion of the total workforce. The pressure to compromise ethical standards, which is often a leading indicator of future misconduct, fell substantially from 13% in 2011 to 9% in 2013. This could be a sign that companies are implementing stronger ethics cultures in their workplaces.

While the NBES report expresses an overall positive view of current ethical behavior in business, it also expresses a number of warnings. A relatively high percentage of misconduct (60%) is committed by people having some level of managerial authority—"the very people who are supposed to set a good example of ethical conduct and make sure that employees honor company rules," says the report. And 24% of observed unethical behavior involved senior managers. Patricia Harned, ERC president, says that managers should be held to a higher standard: "The nature of [observed] misdeeds is alarming. A strong majority of misconduct is attributable to individuals who hold some level of management responsibility. If allowed to persist, rule breaking by managers bodes ill for ethics cultures, because managers set the tone for everyone else."

Equally troubling is that 41% of observed misconduct was committed by multiple people and represented an ongoing pattern within an organization—which means they weren't just isolated incidents. About 12% of misconduct was identified as "companywide," suggesting that the organization had deeper ethical issues. The types of misconduct characterized as companywide were:

- Offering something of value (e.g., cash, gifts, entertainment) to customers/clients (24%);

- Health/safety violations (22%);

- Offering something of value to public officials (20%);

- Violating employee benefits, wage, or overtime rules (20%); and

- Violating internet policies (20%). The percentage of workers who decided to blow the whistle on misconduct they observed fell slightly to 63% from 65% in 2011 after consistently rising in previous NBESs. Being silent about misconduct enables workplace culture to erode with bad behavior.

The percentage of whistleblowers who experienced retaliation after reporting wrongdoing declined from 22% in 2011 to 21% in 2013. This is still disturbingly high since fear of retaliation is a key concern that workers cite for remaining silent when observing wrongdoing. Harned stated, "Reducing retaliation rates is one of the most important challenges facing businesses as they strive for strong ethics cultures."

The ERC believes that increasingly sophisticated ethics and compliance programs are likely to result in improved worker conduct. And the report found more evidence that many companies are taking a proactive approach to creating a strong ethical culture:

- The percentage of companies providing ethics training rose from 74% to 81% between 2011 and 2013.

- Two-thirds of companies (67%) included ethical conduct as a performance measure in employee evaluations, up from 60% in 2011.

- Almost three out of four companies (74%) communicated internally about disciplinary actions when wrongdoing occurs.

A possible explanation for some of the differing views contained in the NBES and the GECS reports may be that each surveyed a different population. NBES results are based on responses from 6,420 workers in U.S. businesses (responses from workers in government and the not-for-profit sectors were excluded). On the other hand, the GECS included 5,128 respondents from more than 95 countries, with only 115 responses from the U.S. The U.S. responses also indicated that their perspective was a global footprint and much of their concern for fraud is directed to their operations in "at risk" countries rather than in domestic operations.

While the NBES report showed some favorable trends and developments, the level of unethical actions is still disturbing. That and the results from the GECS report demonstrate the continued need for companies to place greater emphasis on developing, maintaining, and enforcing a strong ethical culture. According to a study from the IBM Institute for Business Value, fraud is estimated to cost companies around the world a total of $3.5 trillion each year. It's time to start reducing that total.

Top-Management Example and Peer Pressures Bring Benefits

Two research studies show how the power of pressures triggered by the actions of top and middle management bring significant benefits to organizations. *The Importance of Ethical Culture: Increasing Trust and Driving Down Risks* and *Ethics and Employee Engagement* are reports published in mid-2010 by the Ethics Resource Center (ERC), a private, nonprofit organization devoted to independent research and the advancement of high ethical standards and practices in public and private institutions.

The latest reports analyze in a new way the data gathered in the Center's 2009 National Business Ethics Survey® (NBES). The NBES is a biennial random telephone survey of adults currently employed at least 20 hours per week for a company with at least two employees. Those working in the governmental sector are eliminated from the survey results.

Consistent with the results of NBES studies in previous years, both of the latest ERC reports link a strong ethical culture to a number of favorable workplace outcomes. A strong ethical culture is associated with both a reduction in observed wrongdoing and an increase in employee engagement. Basically, the ethical culture uses both formal and informal methods to teach employees how things really get done around the organization. To measure ethical culture, ERC has developed indexes that measure employee perceptions of management and supervisory commitment to open and honest communication, positive ethical role modeling, and accountability.

The *Increasing Trust* report notes that fewer instances of observed wrongdoing by employees result in lower organizational risks. These include damage to reputation, deterioration in relationships with customers, loss of valued employees, and even criminal prosecution and fines. The *Employee Engagement* study indicates that increased employee engagement results in highly motivated employees who work more productively, require less supervision, and adapt their efforts more easily to changing roles and responsibilities.

Specific findings concerning wrongdoing in the workplace show that in a strong ethical culture only 4% of employees feel pressure to compromise standards and commit misconduct, compared to 15% in a weaker culture—almost four times greater. Rates of observed

misconduct in strong cultures are roughly half (39%) as high as those in weaker cultures (76%). Failure to report observed misconduct in a strong culture (28%) is less than two-thirds of that in weaker cultures (43%). The retaliation against reporters of misconduct is six times greater in weaker cultures (24%) compared to strong ones (4%).

Ethical leadership by top management is the principal driver of a strong and responsible management style. But a strong coworker culture is associated with the greatest favorable difference in the level of observed financial misconduct. Worrisome financial activities include misappropriating assets, misrepresenting the financial health of the company, violating contracts, and so forth. Only 8% of employees in stronger coworker cultures reported financial misconduct compared to 31% reported in weaker cultures. In other words, stronger cultures cut observations of financial misconduct by three-quarters.

The recent reports revealed some interesting characteristics and trends in workplace culture. The percentage of employees who characterized the ethical culture of their organization as either strong or strong-leaning was higher in 2009 (62%) than in any of the five previous biennial studies. A high percentage of employees (68%) also felt positive about the ethics of their coworkers, but perceptions of the strength of the ethics of supervisors (70%) and top management (66%) are declining from levels in earlier years. Consistent with other research, top managers were reported to be more optimistic about the strength of the culture in their organization than lower-level employees. Eighty-two percent of top managers consider their culture to be strong or strong-leaning compared to 56% of first-line supervisors. Demographic factors are also important in determining the strength of ethical culture. Highly unionized workforces tend to have weaker cultures. Companies with 500 or more employees and are publicly owned were also reported to be at a disadvantage.

Specific findings in *Employee Engagement* document the strong correlation between ethical culture—particularly at the top management and supervisor levels—and employee engagement. In addition to providing greater productivity and lowering costs, engaged employees are more stable and aware that prospects for continuing employment, career development, and advancement depend on their companies' health and stability.

Employees who witnessed misconduct were less engaged than those who didn't. Only 61% of employees who witnessed misconduct displayed high levels of engagement compared to 85% of those who didn't witness wrongdoing. Concerning the most serious violations, higher proportions were seen by disengaged employees. Seventy-three percent of employees who witnessed bribery of a public official, 67% who witnessed environmental violations, 67% who saw misrepresentation of financial information, 60% who saw anticompetitive practices, and 60% who observed insider trading were all disengaged.

Engaged employees (67%) are more likely to report misconduct when they witness it than other employees (57%). Observed but not reported misconduct by disengaged employees means that management is less able to quickly assess and resolve issues. Unreported misconduct can be a huge liability for the organization. Surmise how different the future of BP PLC would have been if it had had a culture of reporting maintenance shortfalls and meaningful testing of safety procedures.

The *Employee Engagement* report summarizes the implications of the research on ethical culture for managers. These findings have several implications for leaders who want to increase productivity, decrease turnover, reduce misconduct, and lessen ethics risk:

- Adopt leadership training that highlights management behaviors that will inspire and motivate employees to be highly effective and efficient—while upholding the company's ethical standards.

- Ensure that ethics resources—such as hotlines/helplines, procedural justice systems, and standards of conduct—are available to management and employees and that those resources are effectively designed, implemented, and promoted.

- Encourage the human resources and ethics and compliance functions to coordinate efforts and initiatives to maximize the effectiveness of both roles.

- In order to identify areas of weakness and promote accountability, regularly assess both the level of employee engagement and the ethical culture of the company.

- Actively and overtly strive to make decisions and act in ways that promote employee engagement and demonstrate the importance of ethics and ethical standards.

In summary, maintaining a strong ethical culture is an important contributor to successful achievement of organizational objectives. It not only improves employee performance, but it helps avoid risks that could result in jeopardy.

Training Is Critical for a Strong Ethical Culture

Ethics training throughout an organization is believed to be a critical determinant of the effectiveness and strength of its corporate culture. The U.S. Sentencing Guidelines (USSG) Manual, for example, considers training to be one of the seven characteristics of an effective ethics and compliance program. Section 8B2.1 of the 2013 *Guidelines Manual* states: "The organization shall take reasonable steps to communicate periodically and in a practical manner its standards and procedures, and other aspects of the compliance and ethics program…by conducting effective training programs and otherwise disseminating information."

To enable organizations to enhance the effectiveness of their training and other ethics efforts, Navex Global, an independent vendor of ethics and compliance services, published its *2014 Ethics and Compliance Training Benchmark Report.* It's based on 763 responses to a survey of management-level ethics and compliance professionals responsible for training throughout their organizations. A strong majority of the responses (88%) were from U.S.-based companies. One-third of the companies surveyed had fewer than 500 employees.

The study found that 94% of decision makers say that the major objective of ethics and compliance programs is evolving from one of legal defensibility to that of "creating a culture of ethics and respect." This signals a growing awareness of employees' need to understand what it means to act ethically and with integrity. There is a realization at all levels of the organization that a culture of ethics and integrity does in fact lead to favorable compliance behaviors. More organizations are recognizing that ethics drives compliance with codes of conduct, laws, and other portions of the compliance program and reduces many kinds of risk within an organization.

To achieve the objective of changing the overall ethics culture, the report calls for high-quality, engaging training combined with other elements of a holistic and robust compliance program. Training that consists of little more than "checking the box" to indicate compliance isn't likely to be effective. The No. 1 training objective, as determined by respondents, is creating a culture of ethics and respect (90%),

followed by compliance with laws and regulations (89%) and prevention of future issues or misconduct (82%).

The report cites concerns of a perceived gap in reaching the training needs of supervisors and managers. About 54% of respondents feel that existing training for their supervisors and managers isn't effective for avoiding missteps. Mishandling or downplaying employee complaints (46%) and undermining commitment to ethics and compliance (38%) also are concerns.

The challenges to overall success include scarcity of available training time (56%), difficulty measuring program effectiveness (54%), and budget limitations (42%). An emerging strategy designed to mitigate money and time constraints is the employment of short-form training called "burst learning." This lets organizations cover more topics in the same training time, resulting in lower costs and providing more frequent opportunities to raise awareness of critical knowledge and refresh previous knowledge. Shorter training modules keep employees engaged when covering topics that might not be stimulating or interesting to them.

The reported average amount of training provided to employees is six hours annually, with 76% of organizations offering five or fewer hours. Small organizations deliver more training than large organizations—three more hours annually. Members of boards of directors receive one hour of annual training, and third parties don't get any.

Training Is Critical for a Strong Ethical Culture

Respondents reported on the training topic priorities their organizations have planned for the next two to three years, which include ethics and code of conduct (85%), workplace harassment (79%), conflicts of interest (68%), and confidential information (66%). Responding organizations use a wide variety of training formats, including online interactive, live group, and email. A typical curriculum consists of about six topics, which provides variety to reach and engage key audiences. Quality is the most important factor in assuring productivity in ethics and compliance programs as various instructional formats and approaches differ in effectiveness.

Overall, the most important training efforts should focus on code of conduct and harassment training since these are the two greatest risks organizations face. Also, training should be thoughtfully matched to address the most important risk areas specific to each organization.

Overcoming the Fraud Triangle

The Financial Executives Research Foundation (FERF) recently published the results of its surveys of financial executives, managers, and staff. The report, *Breaking the Cycle of Fraud,* recommends strategies to mitigate wrongdoing in the two areas of the fraud triangle that are most closely connected to ethical matters: financial pressure and rationalization.

The fraud triangle was created by criminology researchers Edwin Sutherland and Donald Cressey to describe the three elements that come together when an individual commits fraud:

- Opportunity (weak internal controls) allows the fraud to occur.
- Financial pressure (motive) is the perceived need for committing the fraud.
- Rationalization (weak ethics) is the mind-set of the fraudster that justifies the crime.

By imposing stronger internal controls and processes, companies can take specific, visible action to reduce the risk of opportunity. But financial pressure and rationalization closely involve individuals' ethical framework and organizational culture, and those are much more difficult to influence overtly and directly.

Financial Pressure

Breaking the Cycle reiterates the widely described importance of a positive tone at the top of the organization in mitigating financial pressure. The report describes numerous historical examples where a pressured corporate culture brought ruin. In these cases, achieving short-term financial performance targets for bonus purposes was given far higher priority by senior executives than was acting ethically and considering the sustainability of the enterprise.

A resulting ethical culture of failure to "walk the talk" permeates the attitudes of lower-level executives and employees who are likely to do almost anything to please their bosses—even if it violates provisions in the organization's code of conduct as well as their own personal ethical standards.

It doesn't seem like companies are expanding performance goals to avoid this trap. On April 29, 2015, the Securities & Exchange Commission announced a proposed rule to require companies to disclose "the relationship between executive pay and a company's financial performance." The new rule is intended to help shareholders be better informed when electing directors and voting on executive compensation. The metric chosen to represent company performance is total shareholder return (TSR) calculated on an annual basis and compared to the TSR of a peer group of companies. But this rule will only reinforce the existing focus on short-term financial goals and targets. Performance measurements for rewarding senior executives and others should be expanded to include accomplishment of more ethics-based matter.

Rationalization

The FERF report lists a number of important aspects of an effective ethical culture that strengthen efforts to avoid rationalization of improper behavior. These include useful ethics training tailored to the organization, annual surveys of employee attitudes, and effective whistleblowing programs. The training should involve all levels of the organization. It should contain real-world examples of the negative consequences of unethical behavior, be based on the organization's code of ethics, and include true-to-life applications. Other research has shown that in-person training is likely to be most effective.

The annual surveys of employee attitudes and evaluations of the ethical climate recommended by *Breaking the Cycle* must be professionally designed to avoid leading questions. Surveys must also be administered anonymously to encourage truthful responses that will be helpful in assessing the ethical climate of the organization and the effectiveness of the ethics program. Otherwise, the effort could backfire.

If administered properly, whistleblower or helpline programs are extremely important in detecting and deterring unethical behavior in an organization. The 2014 biannual survey by the Association of Certified Fraud Examiners (ACFE) reports that the most common method through which occupational fraud and abuse is revealed (40%) is tips. This is "more than twice the rate of any other detection method. Employees accounted for nearly half of all tips that led to the discovery of fraud," according to the report.

Encourage Whistleblowing

The Anti-Fraud Collaboration reported in 2014 that many employees are hesitant to report wrongdoing internally using their organization's reporting process. The reasons for hesitating are because they have a significant fear of retaliation or because they believe that senior management is involved or won't take any action to stop unethical behavior. There are some legal protections for whistleblowers in some states and some industries. This is why the *IMA Statement of Ethical Professional Practice* recommends that individuals having an ethical conflict should consult their own attorney—not someone affiliated with their employer—regarding their legal obligations and rights.

Ethics training should include motivation for everyone in the organization, as well as suppliers, to utilize the helpline when warranted. Some of the features of a well-designed whistleblower helpline include wide access with global language capability and adaptation to local customs, if necessary; a single helpline for all ethics-related issues; protocols for handling any reports professionally, including documented formal processes for timely investigation and procedures for confidential reporting of results; and formal data security and document retention policies.

The *IMA Statement* requires that all members "shall encourage others within their organization to act in accordance with its overarching principles: Honesty, Fairness, Objectivity, and Responsibility." Have you done your share of encouragement lately?

The Importance of Trust

Research studies have consistently shown that companies with a strong ethical and trusting culture are more profitable than those without it. Prospective employees want to work for a company with a reputation for treating its stakeholders fairly, which leads to greater productivity and lower turnover and training costs. Many customers also prefer to patronize more ethical companies, which results in higher sales and wider margins.

The importance of trust in financial services is exemplified by the number of trust indices in that industry. For example, in 2014 Thomson Reuters used proprietary data and analysis of business news to "track the state of trust" in the top 50 global financial institutions. And Nottingham University Business School produces a Trust and Fairness Index of the financial services industry in the United Kingdom through its Centre for Risk, Banking and Financial Services. Its 2016 report shows that "consumer perceptions of the trustworthiness and fairness of [financial] advisers and brokers have deteriorated 'significantly' in recent months."

Global Measure of Trust

The Edelman Trust Barometer (ETB), which surveyed 33,000 respondents in 28 countries for its 2016 ETB, is the most comprehensive global measure of the level of trust that an institution will "do what is right." The ETB reports "a yawning trust gap" between those who are "elite," or higher-income, more informed, and more educated (15% of the sample), and those in the general population. The four areas studied, from most to least trusted, are nongovernmental organizations, business, media, and government.

This year the overall trust level for these institutions increased two percentage points among the general population, but it still represents less than half (48%) of that population sample. In contrast, the level to which the elites trust institutions grew by four points to 60%, so the overall trust gap widened to 12 percentage points (19 points in the United States).

The ETB reports that the trust differential correlates with income inequality. For example, the U.S. trust level in the highest (71%) and lowest (40%) quartiles of income results in the world's widest trust gap of 31 points. ETB believes that business leaders are too focused on short-term financial results and lobbying efforts rather than on what the general population wants, which is more emphasis on local job creation and other longer-term outcomes.

Business is in the best position to diminish the trust gap— respondents in 21 of 28 countries trust business more than government to solve problems. Eight in 10 think that business can improve socioeconomic conditions in its community while still earning sustainable profits. Among the issues respondents suggest that business should address are access to education and training, access to healthcare, protecting the environment, improving human and civil rights, addressing income inequality, maintaining a modern infrastructure, and reducing poverty.

Increasing Trust

Barbara Brooks Kimmel, founder of Trust Across America-Trust Around the World (TAA-TAW), calls trust "a natural byproduct of strong core values" and also "the outcome of promises kept." TAA-TAW, an organization whose mission is to help enhance trustworthy behavior in organizations, is developing a new framework for analyzing the core drivers of trust and identifying and selecting "high trust" publicly held companies. The framework's acronym is FACTS: Financial stability and strength, Accounting conservativeness, Corporate integrity, Transparency, and Sustainability. TAA-TAW named Texas Instruments, Inc. (TI) as the most trustworthy public company for the period 2010-2014.

The Importance of Trust

Many other organizations are involved in measuring, publicizing, and helping to increase trust in business, government, and society. Perhaps the best-known global organization surveying workplace trust is the Great Place to Work® Institute (GPTW), which produces research for lists of "best workplaces" in publications in 40 countries around the world. The research is based primarily on GPTW's annual Trust Index Employee Survey, which is taken by millions of employees worldwide.

Fortune magazine uses GPTW data to publish the U.S. list of 100 best companies to work for, as well as top companies in a number of subdivisions. Heading 2016 is Alphabet, Inc., the parent company of Google. Google has been leading the list for seven of the last 10 years. Large company leaders selected by GPTW in other countries are less well known. The Gustavson Brand Trust Index surveys the role trust plays in the minds of Canadian consumers and in 2016 found restaurant chain Tim Hortons to be the "most trusted" brand.

GPTW's website notes that "the foundation of every great workplace is trust between employees and management." Robert Levering, GPTW's cofounder, says, "A great place to work is one in which you trust the people you work for, have pride in what you do, and enjoy the people you work with." He adds that "in such environments, people cooperate, innovate and work smarter, which leads to outstanding customer service, higher profits, and greater productivity."

These lists and organizations are important external measures of the work that is or should be done in organizations of all types. For those of us in accounting and finance, trust is an integral part of our profession and our own work. Following the overarching principles of honesty, fairness, objectivity, and responsibility in the *IMA Statement of Ethical Professional Practice,* we can become strong contributors to a culture of trust in our organizations and create positive change from within.

Is Non-GAAP Reporting Unethical?

The constant pressure to report favorable earnings performance motivates many companies to report income numbers that exclude unusual events that almost always seem to be costly and depress earnings. For many years, the use of financial performance measures other than Generally Accepted Accounting Principles (GAAP) has been an important subject to investors and the Securities & Exchange Commission (SEC).

In 1973, the SEC issued Accounting Series Release (ASR) No. 142, "Conditions for Use of Non-GAAP Financial Measures," warning of possible investor confusion from the use of financial measures outside of GAAP. This release states: "If accounting net income computed in conformity with [GAAP] is not an accurate reflection of economic performance for a company or an industry, it is not an appropriate solution to have each company independently decide what the best measure of its performance should be and present that figure to its shareholders as Truth."

One of the objectives of the Sarbanes-Oxley Act of 2002 (SOX) was to "eliminate the manipulative or misleading use of non-GAAP financial measures and, at the same time, enhance the comparability associated with the use of that information." Consequently, the SEC issued Regulation G, "Conditions for Use of Non-GAAP Financial Measures," in January 2003. It requires companies using a non-GAAP measure to disclose that the measure isn't misleading and to provide a reconciliation between their measure and the most directly comparable GAAP measure. The GAAP presentation must have equal or greater prominence. Management must disclose the reasons why the non-GAAP measure provides useful information to investors and offer a statement of additional purposes for which the non-GAAP measure is used. Only GAAP financial information can be presented directly on the face of a company's financial statements, possibly to highlight the fact that the independent audit opinion doesn't cover such information.

Adjusting Earnings

Aside from excluding unusual events for reporting to the public, another prominent use of non-GAAP earnings performance has been to determine executive compensation. Since the passage of the Revenue Reconciliation Act of 1993, executive salaries amounting to more than $1 million aren't tax deductible, but bonus payments of any amount are deductible if they result from achieving established performance goals. A February 26, 2014, article in The Wall Street Journal, "Some Companies Alter the Bonus Playbook," notes that more U.S. companies are using nonstandard accounting measures to compute bonus payments.

For example, Exelon Corporation used non-GAAP earnings to pump up executive bonuses significantly. Its 2012 audited earnings per share (EPS), based on GAAP, were $1.42. To arrive at the publicly reported, adjusted non-GAAP operating EPS of $2.85, management made 10 separate adjustments that amounted to a net increase of $1.43 per share, a little more than 100%. Adjustments that increased non-GAAP EPS included plant retirements and divestitures ($0.29), merger and integration costs ($0.31), State of Maryland commitments related to merger ($0.28), amortization of commodity contract intangibles ($0.93), and Federal Energy Regulatory Commission (FERC) settlement ($0.21). These adjustments increased EPS by $2.02. The adjustments that decreased Exelon's non-GAAP EPS included mark-to-market impact of economic hedging activities ($0.38), unrealized gains related to nuclear decommissioning trust funds ($0.07), and reassessment of state deferred income taxes ($0.14). The total decrease amounted to $0.59. But the EPS used for bonus purposes was $2.91. In other words, Exelon added $0.06 arbitrarily.

Perhaps the most outrageous use of a misleading non-GAAP earnings measure to improve profits was when Groupon, Inc. reported earnings in its initial public offering (IPO) in 2011. It invented a unique measure called "adjusted consolidated segment operating income (CSOI)." The biggest difference from GAAP earnings was online marketing expenses. The rationale for omitting such seemingly normal and recurring expenses wasn't clear in the registration statement, despite the SEC's rule requiring disclosure of the reason non-GAAP information is more informative to investors.

A sample of online earnings press releases from 2013 shows the variety of ways that large and recognizable public companies are describing the costs and expenses they have excluded from their GAAP earnings to arrive at improved non-GAAP performance (see Table 1). Some highlights include Callaway Golf Company, which not only excluded charges related to cost-reduction initiatives as well as gains and sales related to sales of certain brands or products transitioned to a third-party model, but it also presented sales on a constant currency basis and calculated taxes at an assumed rate.

Electronic Arts excluded acquisition-related expenses, amortization of debt discount, certain nonrecurring litigation expenses, change in deferred net revenue (e.g., packaged goods, digital content), loss (gain) on strategic investments, restructuring charges, stock-based compensation, and income tax adjustments. And Gannett Company excluded special items consisting of workforce restructuring charges, transformation costs, pension settlement charges, a noncash impairment charge, a currency-related loss recognized in other nonoperating items, and certain credits to its income tax provision.

Gannett says it believes that such expenses and credits aren't indicative of normal ongoing operations and thus reasons that their inclusion in results makes it more difficult to compare results between periods and with peer group companies. On the contrary, there is likely to be less comparability than if everyone used only GAAP, which is well known and understood, because companies in Gannett's peer group are likely to calculate their own non-GAAP measures in their own way.

A Broken System

Several conclusions seem obvious about the relevance and usability of the current financial reporting system. Even considering the imprecise nature of current accounting standards, it's too easy for companies to turn poor GAAP earnings into great non-GAAP earnings by simply designing their own performance measures that can readily be adjusted to unethically report successful accomplishment of the goals created using those same measures. Consequently, non-GAAP earnings reporting should be strictly limited and permitted only in extraordinary circumstances—that is, in cases where current GAAP doesn't clearly reflect economic reality. Companies should have to demonstrate a real necessity and communicate meaningful, unique reasons why they believe using a non-GAAP measure is mandatory to avoid misleading investors and others, not just to portray better short-term profits, earn bigger bonuses, and cash in on stock options. The widespread use of non-GAAP performance measures seems to provide conclusive evidence that the current financial reporting system is broken. Neither the SEC's December 2013 "Report on Review of Disclosure Requirements in Regulation S-K" nor the February 25, 2014, Financial Accounting Standards Board (FASB) news release, "Post Implementation Review Concludes Fair Value Accounting Standard Meets Its Objectives," addresses the need for basic reporting reform.

The Public Company Accounting Oversight Board (PCAOB) should reconsider Release No. 2012-004, which states, "The auditor's responsibility with respect to information in a document does not extend beyond the financial information identified in his report, and the auditor has no obligation to perform any procedures to corroborate other information contained in a document." Perhaps the responsibility should extend further. Companies spend hundreds of millions of dollars each year to prepare GAAP-based financial statements and to have them audited. These large expenditures don't seem to be worth it if more and more investors and others rely on less reliable non-GAAP disclosures instead.

Table 1: Arriving at Non-GAAP EPS - Company Items Excluded

Analog Devices – Items of a nonrecurring or noncash nature

Anixter International – Acquisitions, foreign exchange effects, impact of copper prices

Baker Hughes – Loss on devaluation of Venezuelan currency

Callaway Golf Company – Gains and sales related to sales of certain brands or products transitioned to a third-party model, charges related to cost-reduction initiatives

Cardinal Health, Inc. – Restructuring and employee severance, acquisition-related costs, impairments and loss on disposal of assets, litigation (recoveries)/charges, net and other spin-off costs

Dell Inc. – Amortization of purchased intangibles, severance, and facility-actions, acquisition-related charges, costs incurred in fiscal 2014 related to Dell's proposed merger, other items

Electronic Arts (EA Games) – Acquisition-related expenses, amortization of debt discount, certain nonrecurring litigation expenses, change in deferred net revenue (e.g., packaged goods, digital content), loss (gain) on strategic investments, restructuring charges, stock-based compensation, income tax adjustments

Facebook – Share-based compensation, related payroll tax expenses, income tax adjustments

Gannett Company, Inc. – Special items consisting of workforce restructuring charges, transformation costs, pension settlement charges, a noncash impairment charge, a currency-related loss recognized in other nonoperating items, certain credits to its income tax provision

IBM Corp. – Charges for the amortization of purchased intangible assets, other acquisition-related charges, retirement-related charges driven by changes to plan assets, liabilities primarily related to market performance

Ingram-Micro, Inc. – Charges associated with restructuring, integration, and transition costs and other expense reduction programs, amortization expense associated with intangible assets, gains due to the foreign-currency translation effect on euro-based inventory purchases in the company's pan-European entity

Merck & Co., Inc. – Acquisition-related costs, costs related to restructuring programs, certain other items

Microchip Technology Inc. – The effect of share-based compensation, expenses related to acquisition activities (including intangible asset amortization; inventory valuation costs; severance costs; earn-out adjustments; and legal, general, and administrative expenses associated with acquisitions), nonrecurring tax events, noncash interest expense on convertible debentures

WGL Holdings, Inc. – The effects of unrealized mark-to-market gains (losses) on energy-related derivatives for regulated utility and retail energy marketing segments, certain gains and losses associated with optimizing the utility segment's system capacity assets, changes in the measured value of inventory for wholesale energy solutions segment, the financial effects of warm or cold weather that exceeds weather protection for the regulated utility segment, certain unusual transactions

Williams-Sonoma – Unusual business events

Yahoo! – Stock-based compensation

Benchmarking Ethics and Compliance Programs

One of the questions asked most frequently by those involved in corporate ethics responsibility is "How are we doing?" The question raised is how an organization stacks up in comparison with what it should do. Intended to form the basis of best practices in ethics and compliance, *Foundation Guidelines "Red Book": Application Draft, April 2005,* is an online document published by the Open Compliance and Ethics Group (OCEG). This framework document, available at www.oceg.org, details the essential components of an integrated compliance and ethics program and is intended to provide guidelines and benchmarks for:

- Integrated Governance, Compliance, Risk Management, and Ethics
- Mission, Vision, Values
- Compliance and Ethics Programs
- Whistleblower Hotlines
- Codes of Conduct/Ethics
- Compliance and Ethics Training Programs
- Program Audit, Assessment, and Benchmarking

Publication of the OCEG guidance is especially timely considering that the U.S. Sentencing Commission raised the bar on ethics and compliance programs last year by upgrading the necessity for organizations to monitor and oversee the effectiveness of their program to the board of directors level. The Sentencing Commission amendment applies to nonprofit organizations as well as public and privately held corporations.

The OCEG framework document demonstrates how to integrate good governance practices, risk management, ethics, and compliance into normal business operating practices. According to the OCEG, benefits from an effective ethics and compliance program include avoidance of social, reputational, and economic risks and civil liability as well as possible criminal penalties. The six principles that permeate the framework are:

1. **Integrate Compliance and Ethics.** The set of core values intrinsic to the company should be mirrored in its commitment to ethics and compliance as well as the design of the program and how it operates.

2. **Embed Compliance and Ethics Management Processes into the Business.**

3. **Demonstrate Leadership.** The tone at the top is critical, so senior management should consistently put the organization's values into practice and clearly communicate the program's expectations to all employees. Periodic appraisal of employee integrity and ethical behavior should be included as part of the normal performance evaluation process.

4. **Require Accountability and Ownership.** The compliance and ethics program should motivate a culture within the organization that recognizes the premise that individuals should be responsible for their actions.

5. **Provide an Open Culture.** Opportunities must be provided for employees to speak up about sensitive issues without being afraid of negative reaction.

6. **Measure Performance and Results.** Results of periodic evaluation of the program's performance should be used to make improvements.

The components of the OCEG guidance framework structure include four elements: culture, planning, responding, and evaluating. Culture is the central aspect of an ethics and compliance program, according to OCEG, and it is surrounded by the other three. When establishing a new ethics and compliance program, the first step should be for management to have a full understanding of the organization's culture. Typically, elements within culture are deeply embedded behaviors that may not be easy to change. But making necessary changes in the culture of an organization can be the key factor in ensuring success of an ethics and compliance program. The four types of culture that must be considered are ethical culture, governance culture, risk culture, and human capital culture.

The OCEG framework lists the other three components—planning, responding, and evaluating—as necessary to implement. The planning step outlines the objectives of the ethics and compliance program and helps align the program with the objectives of the organization. The responding step defines the elements in the program that are necessary to reacting properly to risks and opportunities. The evaluation step provides for continuous-loop feedback that allows for improvements to be made when and where necessary. Evaluation should be the first step when modifying an existing ethics and compliance program.

Each component of the OCEG framework contains a number of topics, and each topic may contain as many as six entries. These can include:

- Description: the context and importance of a particular guideline
- Legal Requirements: actions required by law or regulation
- Standards/Guidance: actions required or recommended in key documents of other organizations
- Core Practices: recommended ways to satisfy requirements or recommendations
- Advanced Practices: enhanced methods appropriate for some organizations
- Sources: citations to the source of requirements, recommendations, or actions

As another part of its efforts, OCEG has published a questionnaire titled *Does the Company Get It?* This 20-question document, available on OCEG's website and presented with its permission, is designed to determine whether a company has an effective process and culture in place to control and mitigate compliance and ethics-related risks. Included with each of the 20 questions are answers to why the question should be asked, potential answers to the question, and potential difficulties or red flags. The 20 questions are:

1. What does your organization say about compliance, ethics, and values in its formal mission and vision statement?

2. How do your board and management set the "tone at the top" and communicate compliance and ethics values, mission, and vision?

3. How do you know if your employees and other stakeholders are "convinced" that the organization is serious about its compliance and ethics responsibilities?

4. What is the scope of your compliance and ethics program, and how does it integrate with your overall business strategy?

5. How do you assess compliance and ethics risks, and how does this process integrate with enterprise risk management (ERM)?

6. What position in the organization provides oversight and leadership in the compliance/ethics function, and where does this position fall in the organizational chart?

7. What is the organizational structure of your compliance and ethics management team?

8. How are resources allocated for compliance and ethics management activities—both routinely and to address significant issues that arise?

9. What does your Code of Conduct address, and who receives it?

10. How do you distribute your Code of Conduct and confirm that employees both receive and understand the Code and other policies?

11. What is your process for updating policies/procedures?

12. Can any requirements established by the Code of Conduct and other policies be waived or overridden, and, if so, what is the process for doing so?

13. How often and by what methods does your management communicate the values, mission, and vision of the compliance and ethics program to employees and other stakeholders?

14. Do you provide comprehensive training and conduct performance evaluations for each job role to ensure compliance and ethics responsibilities are understood and followed and that necessary skills are learned and employed?

15. How do employees, agents, and other stakeholders raise issues regarding compliance and ethics-related matters?

16. How do you handle compliance and ethics issues that arise and scrutinize the sources of compliance failures?

17. How consistently and in what way have you taken action against violators of the Code and programs?

18. What is the process for determining which issues are escalated to the board and for informing the board when issues are resolved?

19. What ongoing processes are in place to monitor the effectiveness of the compliance and ethics program?

20. Does the organization engage an external law firm or consultant to audit compliance and ethics program elements?

Question:

Does your organization have an effective ethics and compliance program?

Economic Crime Results from Unethical Culture

PricewaterhouseCoopers has released its fourth biannual study on the cause and existence of fraud. Perhaps the most extensive global study of its kind, the *2007 Global Economic Crime Survey* provides an in-depth look at the root causes of economic crime and the ways in which it affects businesses worldwide.

The most important finding in the study is that it shows how it's nearly impossible to get rid of economic crime. The report asserts that the many types of fraud and the broad range of perpetrators make eliminating fraud an impossible task. In terms of deterrence, the study concludes that improved systems and controls are important but insufficient. A strong ethical climate is equally important in preventing fraudulent activities from occurring.

The results of the study, based on personal interviews with 5,400 companies in 40 countries, provide an eight-year perspective on the increases in the amount and types of economic crime. The statistics reported in the *2007 Global Economic Crime Survey* show a continued high incidence of economic crime. Half of the companies surveyed fell victim to some type of economic crime in the past two years despite increased attention to systems and controls. The current overall level is nearly constant in the last two years and is a 6% increase over 2003. The highest levels of fraud were reported in Africa, North America, and Central-Eastern Europe.

Of the types of economic crime, asset misappropriation is the only category perceived to have become less of a threat. Even so, it was still the largest category of economic crime, and the number of companies that reported experiencing asset misappropriation incidents increased modestly over the eight-year period. The other categories, which include accounting fraud, money laundering, intellectual property infringement, and corruption and bribery, saw increases in the number of reported incidents as well as the threat of occurrences.

The report concludes that the recent emphasis on controls designed to assure proper external financial reporting fails to consider the other types of fraud risks. Further, all controls need to be constantly upgraded and improved to thwart the efforts of fraudsters who are always seeking ways to circumvent even the most rigorous of control systems. The report suggests that the value of control systems lies in ensuring that controls:

- Reflect the culture of the organization and its ethical guidelines.
- Consistently investigate and deal with all incidents of reported fraud, regardless of the position of the perpetrator inside or outside the firm.
- Are continuously strengthened and upgraded.

The average direct cost of fraud was reported to be $3.2 million per company. Additional costs were incurred through distraction of management, dealing with litigation issues, managing investor relations, and dealing with regulators. There was also collateral damage to the "brand," to staff morale, and to relationships with other stakeholders.

The methods reported for detecting fraud reflect results similar to those of previous studies. Most (41%) were discovered by chance, an increase of 7% in the last two years. Discoveries from a whistleblower hotline tripled to 8% over the period, and 35% were detected from information provided from individuals either inside or outside the organization. Where an anonymous reporting system was judged to be effective, the percentage from this cause almost doubled to 14%. These findings reflect the importance of an anonymous reporting system, such as that required by the Sarbanes-Oxley Act and included in the U.S. Federal Sentencing Guidelines.

In listing the conditions needed to enable fraud, the report uses different language to describe the elements contained in the well-known Fraud Triangle. According to the report, the factors that enable fraud to be committed are perpetrator incentive to commit fraud, perpetrator ability to rationalize its commission, and insufficient controls to prevent fraud occurrence. Additionally, the report maintains that other factors are important in allowing fraud to take place in an organization, including a lack of ethics, values, programs, and systems that discourage fraud. This includes absence of a well-developed ethical culture, which includes systems that encourage and protect employees who expose fraud.

The fraud prevention practices closely mirror the key elements of ethics and compliance programs set forth by the U.S. Federal Sentencing Commission:

- Creating an appropriate control environment that has the right tone and structure:

  - Senior management communication of the importance of ethical behavior and "zero tolerance" of any illegal acts or ethical misconduct;

  - Maintaining a quality compliance organization that is staffed by professionals;

  - Ethics and compliance factors integrated into reward systems and other human resource policies and procedures, including hiring, training, performance, promotion, and disciplinary actions.

- Regularly training all employees in the content and application of the organization's code of conduct.

- Focusing on the most important compliance risks:

  - Performing risk assessments to identify processes with highest risk;

  - Revising policies and procedures to reflect the results of the assessment;

- Regular monitoring of effectiveness of compliance controls.

- Providing assurance of control effectiveness to internal governance structure.

The survey report also contains best-practice suggestions for whistleblowing programs. The most important concepts include:

- **Maintain confidentiality, and protect whistleblowers.** It's essential to encourage employees to report misconduct with the confidence they won't be subject to retaliation in any form. Confidential reporting mechanisms should be readily available and easy to use. A helpline assists employees to understand and apply the code of conduct.

- **Formalize procedures for handling reports of possible misconduct.** Many incidents reported may involve personnel matters and require follow-up with appropriate members of management.

Other incidents may be more serious and require reporting to higher governance levels, including the Audit Committee.

Additional important findings in the study include the need for top-down communication and the exercise of ethical behavior. Accountability at the top for actually living by the code of conduct is critical. In 30% of the cases where an ethics incident involved a member of senior management, there was significant ongoing damage to the morale of the entire employee group. Unfortunately, the study also found that offenders who belonged to senior management were treated differently. Criminal charges were brought less frequently against senior management, and the consequences were usually limited to a warning or reprimand.

In summary, the report finds two key factors that organizations need to focus on to position themselves against the threats of economic crime. The first is an enterprise-wide risk management program that includes continuous proactive monitoring of fraud threat vulnerabilities combined with a comprehensive ethics and compliance program that encompasses all aspects of the organization. The second factor is the development of a strong ethical culture that is known and practiced by employees at every level.

New Survey of Workplace Ethics Shows Surprising Results

The ethical culture of the U.S. workplace is in transition, according to the 2011 *National Business Ethics Survey* (NBES) published by the Washington, D.C.-based Ethics Resource Center (ERC). ERC is a private, nonprofit organization devoted to independent research and the advancement of high ethical standards and practices in public and private organizations. Subtitled *Workplace Ethics in Transition,* this seventh biannual study by the ERC is based on responses from nearly 4,700 employees at all levels working at least 20 hours per week in the for-profit sector. Responses came from interviews conducted online and over the telephone. Data was weighted for gender, age, and education.

Some of the study results are easily understandable, but others are unexpected and surprising. ERC calls the news both "very good" and "very troubling," saying that the findings, "which are unlike any the ERC has seen in its prior surveys, indicate something is driving a shift in the American workplace." According to ERC President Patricia Harned, "While most U.S. workers are currently 'doing the right thing' by following company standards and reporting wrongdoing when they see it, we see trouble ahead." She adds that the 2011 results show "factors that historically indicate that American business may be on the cusp of a large downward shift in ethical conduct."

The state of the economy has always been one of the major causes of workplace misbehavior— companies behave differently during economic difficulties. Because of management actions, employees perceive a heightened commitment to ethics during hard times and adopt a higher standard of behavior. Since job security is low during a downturn, employees tend to be more careful to avoid making mistakes. Consequently, only 45% of U.S. workers report witnessing actual misconduct—an historic, if still somewhat troubling, low. The five most frequently observed misconduct events were misuse of company time (33%), abusive behavior (21%), company resource abuse (20%), lying to employees (20%), and violating corporate internet use policies (16%).

The proportion of employees who observed misconduct and then decided to report it climbed to a record high of 65%. The willingness of employees to say something about what they saw depended significantly on the nature of the violation. The highest proportion of reported violations involved stealing or improper payment offers to public officials—nearly 70% of workers who witnessed such actions reported the violations. Similarly, almost two-thirds of employees reported improper use of competitors' inside information, the falsification of expense reports, trading on inside information, making improper political contributions, delivery of goods or services that failed to meet specifications, abusive behavior or behavior that creates a hostile work environment, and the falsification and/or manipulation of financial reporting information.

On the low reporting side, only 43% of employees who witnessed violations of company internet use policies reported it, and only half reported the inappropriate use of social networking they observed.

In terms of where employees report observed misconduct, supervisors remain the most likely recipient, at 56%. Company hotlines receive only 5% of misconduct reports and external parties only 3%.

Some of the actions that companies have taken to reduce the level of misbehavior and increase the reporting of violations include heightened efforts to raise awareness of ethics (42%) and management watching employee actions more closely (34%). Forty-four percent of employees believe their business is taking fewer risks, and 30% agree that the bad actors in their company are just lying low because of the recession.

Clouding this better news are the "ominous warning signs of a potentially significant ethics decline ahead." The percentage of employees who experienced some form of retaliation for blowing the whistle was 22%, an all-time high. This compares with 15% in 2009 and 12% in 2007. The proportion of respondents who felt they couldn't question management without fear of retaliation amounted to 19% of all employees.

Many of the retaliatory actions were severe:

- Excluded from decisions and work activity by supervisor or management (64%)

- Given a cold shoulder by other employees (62%)

- Verbal abuse by supervisor or someone else in management (62%)

- Almost lost job (56%)

- Not given promotions or raises (55%)

- Verbal abuse by other employees (51%)

- Hours or pay were cut (46%)

- Relocated or reassigned (44%)

- Demoted (32%)

- Experienced online harassment (31%)

- Experienced physical harm to their person or property (31%)

- Harassed at home (29%)

Further, the NBES reported the percentage of employees who perceived pressure to compromise their company's ethical standards or even break the law so they could perform their jobs jumped significantly from 8% in 2009 to 13% in 2011. This is the highest level since 2000.

Another worrisome finding was that the share of companies that employees reported as having a weak ethical culture climbed to near-record levels of 42%, up from 35% in the previous survey two years ago. The NBES measures critical aspects of ethics culture, including management's trustworthiness, whether managers at all levels talk about ethics and model appropriate behavior, and the extent to which employees value and support ethical conduct, accountability, and transparency.

As expected, there's a very strong correlation between a strong ethical culture and lower observed misconduct. Misconduct was observed in only 29% of companies with a strong ethical culture but seen in 90% of those with a weak ethical culture. Pressure to compromise ethical standards was felt in 33% of companies having a weak ethical culture vs. only 7% where the ethical culture was strong. Employees in companies with weak cultures failed to report observed misconduct 48% of the time, but only 6% of employees in companies with strong cultures didn't report misconduct they observed. Retaliation after reporting misconduct was also more prevalent in weaker cultures— 46% vs. 28% in companies with strong cultures.

The 2011 NBES showed declines in both critical drivers of a company's ethical culture—the actions of senior leaders and of supervisors. Confidence in the ethics of senior leaders declined from 68% to 62%, equaling the all-time low reflected in the 2000 study. The proportion of employees who believe their supervisors act as ethical leaders fell from 76% in 2009 to 66% in the latest study. In another sign of weakening ethical cultures, the proportion of employees that said they were confident they could properly handle an ethics situation fell from 86% in 2009 to 77% in 2011.

Because of the increased use of social media in recent years, the 2011 NBES included questions about social networks and active users. These questions provided surprising findings from the experiences of active social networkers—defined as those who spend 30% or more of their workday using social network sites. The ethical experiences of this group are so far outside the range of their colleagues that they had a significant influence on the overall findings.

Comparisons of active social networkers with the remainder of the sample showed networkers experienced far more negative ethical events than their counterparts:

- Observed misconduct: 72% of networkers vs. 54% of the rest

- Felt pressure to compromise standards: 42% vs. 11%

- Experienced retaliation after reporting misconduct: 56% vs. 18%

Even more disturbing, perhaps, are findings that active social networkers appear to believe that many questionable ethical actions are actually acceptable, including:

- Buying personal items with your company credit card as long as you pay it back (42% of networkers believe this is acceptable behavior)

- Doing a little less work to compensate for cuts in benefits or pay (51%)

- Keeping a copy of confidential work documents in case you need them in your next job (50%)

- Taking a copy of work software home and using it on your personal computer (46%)

- "Friending" a client/customer on a social network (59%)

- Blogging or tweeting negatively about your company or colleagues (42%)

- Uploading vacation pictures to the company network or server so you can share them with coworkers (50%)

- Using social networking to find out what your company's competitors are doing (54%)

In summary, the results of the 2011 NBES sound an alarm to business leaders to make strong business ethics a top priority in their strategic plans. The improved results in some areas could also just be a symptom of the current economic situation, and leaders need to remain vigilant about emphasizing the importance of a strong ethical culture and living up to that vision.

Measuring Trust in Business

Trust isn't one of the four overarching ethical principles contained in the *IMA Statement of Ethical Professional Practice,* but it is certainly an inevitable outcome from the application of honesty, fairness, objectivity, and responsibility. Trust underpins the practice of each of those principles, and only with trust can business transactions be entered into with confidence. A company's use of trust as a basic business strategy allows it to demonstrate superior performance on a number of other metrics.

Being able to quantify the trustworthiness of a company would be valuable information to both investors and the general public. Two groups, Governance Metrics International's Audit Integrity (AI) service and Next Decade, Inc.'s Trust Across America™ (TAA) unit, have been attempting to do just that. Both have published lists of the most trustworthy companies in the United States.

Audit Integrity

For the past seven years, the Audit Integrity service of Governance Metrics International has been applying the Accounting and Governance Risk (AGR) rating to identify the existence of factors most associated with fraud and the risks of a decline in stock price. The AGR rating serves as the basis for the *Forbes Risk List* and involves more than 100 factors that attempt to measure the quality of corporate accounting and management practices. AI believes the resulting score demonstrates solid corporate governance and management. Companies must have a market capitalization of $200 million to be considered.

In April 2010, *Forbes* published AI's list of the 100 Most Trustworthy U.S. companies in three categories of market capitalization. In addition to the AGR score, AI's evaluation of trustworthiness uses additional factors that penalize companies for unusual or excessive executive compensation, a high proportion of incentive-based executive pay, high levels of management turnover, substantial insider trading, class action litigation, and restatements or other accounting issues. Fewer than 5% of public companies make AI's Most Trustworthy list.

The nine top-ranked companies—three in each of the large-, mid-, and small-cap categories—based on the average AGR score for the last three calendar quarters are:

- Bed Bath & Beyond, Inc., a $7.8 billion retailer, largely in the U.S. and Canada, specializing in domestics merchandise and home furnishings;

- Enbridge Energy Partners, LP, a $5.7 billion provider of oil well services and equipment;

- Hess Corporation, a $34 billion global integrated energy company;

- Montpelier Re Holdings, Ltd., a $748 million provider of customized reinsurance and insurance solutions;

- Werner Enterprises, Inc., a $1.8 billion global transportation provider of freight management and supply chain solutions;

- Casey's General Stores, Inc., a $4.6 billion owner, operator, and franchisor of convenience stores, largely in the midwestern U.S.;

- Greenlight Capital Re, Ltd., a $415 million Cayman Islands-based open market property and casualty reinsurance company;

- National Interstate Insurance Company, a $309 million insurer specializing in transportation risks; and

- CDI Corporation, a $926 million provider of engineering and information technology, outsourcing solutions, and professional staffing.

Trust Across America

In December 2010, Next Decade, Inc.'s Trust Across America™ unit published its ranking of trustworthy corporations. Based on data from 3,000 public companies, TAA utilizes five indicators of trustworthy corporate business behavior: financial stability and strength, accounting conservativeness, corporate integrity, transparency, and sustainability. Scores on each of these factors are weighted equally. The analysis attempts to identify companies that embed trustworthy business behavior in their corporate culture.

Hess Corporation was named by TAA as the Most Trustworthy Public Company of 2010. The Hess website indicates the company's six core values that represent its collective conscience and are embedded throughout the organization: Integrity, People, Performance, Value Creation, Social Responsibility, and Independent Spirit. Hess says its business is committed to "longstanding relationships built on trust." The company also notes it has received specific recognition for its sustainability efforts.

The other Top 10 companies ranked by TAA in 2010 represent a wide spectrum of industries:

- Albemarle Corporation, a $2.4 billion U.S. producer of specialty chemicals;

- Best Buy, Inc., a $50 billion, largely U.S. specialty retailer of consumer electronics;

- Cummins, Inc., a $10.8 billion global firm that designs, manufactures, distributes, and services engines and related technologies that provide power to various industries;

- Eastman Chemical Company, a $5.8 billion global producer of more than 1,200 chemicals, fibers, and plastics;

- Lexmark International, Inc., a $4 billion global provider of printing and imaging products, software, solutions, and services;

- Lubrizol Corporation, a $1.3 billion global producer and distributor of specialty chemicals;

- Sonoco Products Company, a $4 billion global manufacturer of consumer and industrial packaging and provider of packaging services;

- Texas Instruments Inc., a $14 billion global manufacturer of semiconductors; and

- USANA Health Sciences, a $518 million developer and manufacturer of nutritional supplements, healthy weight management, and self-preserving personal care products that it sells directly through associates to global consumers.

Difficulty in Measuring Trust

Measuring and rating trust isn't an easy, straightforward task, and more work needs to be done in refining how we measure it.

The AI list shows surprising volatility in AGR scores over a short period of time. In August 2010, *Forbes* published updated AGR scores and rankings for the 382 highest-ranked trustworthy companies. Comparison of this list with the April 2010 data shows considerable change in rankings. The apparent instability of AGR scores is somewhat surprising since you wouldn't expect the characteristics being measured—solid governance and good management practices—to vary in such a short period of time. In the August list, AI highlighted 104 (27%) of the 382 companies that had consistently met Most Trustworthy criteria for five years or longer. (To allow analysis from a longer-term perspective, only the rankings of these companies were used for comparison with those on the April list.)

Of the nine described as Most Trustworthy in April, only Hess Corporation survived as one of the 26 highest-ranked in the August list. Werner Enterprises, Inc. and Enbridge Energy Partners remained in the top 10% of companies. National Interstate Insurance Company and CDI Corp. had high scores but hadn't qualified as Most Trustworthy for five years. Casey's General Stores scored much lower, and Bed Bath & Beyond, Montpelier Re Holdings, and Greenlight Capital weren't listed among the 382 highest.

There are two possible explanations for the significant changes in the evaluations of relatively static conditions such as overall trustworthiness: difficulties in measurement or the inability to measure the proper variables. Unlike a number of organizations that prepare lists of "best" companies on varying criteria, AI doesn't ask companies to submit data themselves and appears to use only publicly available data. Consequently, self-selection bias should be minimized.

It's quite possible that the AGR scores reflect the probability of downside risk very well, but the dilemma here is that trustworthiness may not necessarily be the converse of a lack of downside risk. For example, an ineffective board of directors and poor internal controls may well be closely associated with the risk of massive embezzlement, like that experienced by Koss Corporation, but even a highly effective board may not be able to guarantee trustworthiness throughout the organization.

In addition, the differences between the TAA and AI lists show the different approaches and varied opinions regarding the metrics that best indicate a company's trustworthiness. In comparing the two lists, Hess is the only company that appears on both, and none of the other nine TAA selections is included in the AI list of 382 most trustworthy companies.

In the end, both TAA and AI are to be commended for bringing attention to the critically important ethical topic of trust in business. The TAA website says, "Many people believe…that companies across the entire country, and perhaps the world, cannot be trusted." Hopefully, the success of trustworthy organizations will motivate more companies to adopt best practices. As Thomas Friedman wrote in *The World is Flat,* "It is trust that allows us to take down walls, remove barriers, and eliminate friction." Trust allows innovation to occur and the organizations that harbor it to flourish. More effort needs to be expended on setting standards for trustworthiness and measuring them appropriately.

Ethical Behavior for Management Accountants

It's well established that members of the accountancy profession have a responsibility to serve the interests of many stakeholders in society, including those of the general public. For example, the first words of the *Handbook of the Code of Ethics for Professional Accountants* (Handbook) mention the interests of the public: "A distinguishing mark of the accountancy profession is its acceptance of the responsibility to act in the public interest." The Handbook is published annually by the International Ethics Standards Board for Accountants (IESBA), a part of the International Federation of Accountants (IFAC).

IFAC's broad definition of the public interest in *IFAC Policy Position 5* is "the net benefits derived for, and procedural rigor employed on behalf of, all society in relation to any action, decision, or policy." Because the accountancy profession touches on every aspect of society, the public includes all groups and individuals—consumers, investors, taxpayers, and citizens. According to IFAC, determining whether an action, decision, or policy is in the public interest involves two phases: assessing net benefits (to see if benefits outweigh the costs) and considering whether the issue was evaluated with transparency, public accountability, independence, competence, adherence to due process, and participation of a wide range of societal groups.

IMA Ethics Statement

Management accountants in particular have diverse responsibilities to serve the needs of a variety of constituencies. They must maintain the highest standards of ethical conduct while serving the requirements of the organization where they are employed and the public at large. They also must be responsible to themselves and their families while acting in the best long-term interests of the profession as a whole.

IMA® (Institute of Management Accountants) members are required to behave ethically, according to the *IMA Statement of Ethical Professional Practice* (the *Statement*). When joining the organization or renewing, members must commit to complying with the *Statement*, which includes overarching principles that express values as well as standards to guide conduct. The overarching principles include honesty, fairness, objectivity, and responsibility. Members face

disciplinary action for failure to comply with 13 specific standards for competence, confidentiality, integrity, and credibility. Additionally, the *Statement* outlines guidance and specific steps to consider when resolving ethical conflict.

Other Ethics Codes

The Financial Executives International (FEI) *Code of Ethics* contains obligations for its members that are very similar to those in the *IMA Statement*. These include honesty and integrity, completeness of information, compliance with laws, action in good faith and due care, and confidentiality. There are other obligations as well, such as to "proactively promote ethical behavior as a responsible partner among peers, in the work environment and the community" and to "achieve responsible use of and control over all assets and resources employed or entrusted."

The FEI *Code of Ethics* includes the mission of expending "significant efforts to promote ethical conduct in the practice of financial management throughout the world." Further, the FEI code embodies rules "regarding individual and peer responsibilities, as well as responsibilities to employers, the public, and other stakeholders."

The Code of Ethics for internal auditors published by the Institute of Internal Auditors (IIA) contains four principles: integrity, objectivity, confidentiality, and competency. Each has several rules of conduct that prescribe actions that internal auditors must take to remain in compliance with the IIA ethics code. The IIA definition of internal auditing points out that the function is an "independent, objective assurance and consulting activity" within an organization that is "designed to add value and improve an organization's operations."

Finally, the IESBA Handbook contains five fundamental ethical principles with which all professional accountants are expected to comply, including those employed in business. The principles are integrity, objectivity, professional competence and due care, confidentiality, and professional behavior. The Handbook groups threats to compliance with those fundamental principles into one or more of the following categories: self-interest, self-review, advocacy, familiarity, and intimidation.

Safeguards that eliminate those threats or reduce them to an acceptable level may be created through external factors like the profession, legislation, or regulation or through factors internal to the work environment. The underlying approach of the Handbook is to describe how professional accountants should deal with ethical issues by evaluating threats and safeguards. It discusses conflicts of interest and lists steps the professional accountant in business should take if he or she can't resolve an ethical conflict, including resigning from the employing organization.

Accountants in Public Practice

In contrast with those for management accountants, the ethical responsibilities of independent public accountants, particularly those serving publicly held audit clients, are more restricted. Rule 2-01 of the Securities & Exchange Commission (SEC) Regulation S-X was "designed to ensure that auditors are qualified and independent of their audit clients both in fact and in appearance" so that their services are entirely focused on the mission of protecting the interests of investors, creditors, and the general public.

More than 70% of the IESBA Handbook deals with ethical matters important only to accountants in public practice rather than those employed in business. Because of its importance, the subject of independence takes up the bulk of these pages. Other matters covered include professional appointment, conflicts of interest, second opinions, fees and other types of remuneration, marketing professional services, gifts and hospitality, custody of client assets, and objectivity for all services. Although philosophically a principles-based document, the book seems to be full of detailed and prescriptive rules.

Ethics Guidance

As these various codes demonstrate, accountants have a number of sources to draw from when examining the ethics aspect of the profession. The prescriptive, concise communication of specific behavioral standards, as seen in the *IMA Statement of Ethical Professional Practice* and some of the other ethics codes discussed, effectively enables management accountants to act ethically and to consider their responsibilities to all groups in society.

Do Consulting Services Threaten Audit Performance?

The Sarbanes-Oxley Act of 2002 (SOX) prohibits independent auditors from providing to their audit clients specified nonaudit services, primarily management consulting. But auditing firms, including the Big 4, appear to be moving back toward providing more consulting services in order to benefit their bottom line. The ethics culture that drives the deliberate strategy to provide more of these highly profitable and rapidly growing consulting services could very well lead to the same conflict of interest that brought about the SOX legislation—that is, diminished efforts by audit firms to perform high-quality audits for the benefit of investors and the public.

The language in SOX Section 202 specifically bars audit firms from providing to their audit clients consulting services involving "management functions or human resources" and "expert services unrelated to the audit." Yet PricewaterhouseCoopers (PwC) announced in 2013 that it was acquiring Booz & Co., a global full line commercial management consulting firm, closing the deal this past April. With this acquisition, PwC significantly adds to the nearly one-third of total revenue it earns from providing consulting services. Former Securities & Exchange Commission (SEC) Chairman Arthur Levitt said, "We are slipping back. As the accounting profession becomes more committed to consulting, their audit activities have got to be questioned."

PwC's press release broadly describes the purchase of Booz as providing "an enhanced range of services for our clients" and announces the new name for Booz is Strategy& (pronounced "Strategy and"). The release also says that the acquisition "reflects the strength in strategy consulting that Booz & Company brings to the PwC Network and the benefits this deal will bring to all clients and stakeholders." It isn't clear how consulting clients about strategies doesn't expressly conflict with both the language and intent of SOX to preserve the independence of audit firms from their clients.

The website for Strategy& contains information about the types of services the firm provides and articulates what it means by "strategy consulting." Some of the statements on the site include:

- "What PwC and Strategy& create together will be unique."
- "We'll offer clients something they can't get elsewhere: a combination of strategy consulting expertise, and a proven track record of delivery, with unrivalled global scale and experience."

- "Clients will be able to get practical strategy advice from people who understand the opportunities and risks involved in implementation—and strategic execution skills from people who understand the context."

These suggest that one of PwC's primary growth strategies is to provide broad-scope consulting that involves the kinds of strategic business decisions only management and the board of directors can make and then facilitate the tactical implementation of those decisions.

In a May 1, 2014, speech at Baruch College's 13th Annual Financial Reporting Conference, James R. Doty, chairman of the Public Company Accounting Oversight Board (PCAOB), noted that "Audit is a declining portion of accounting firms' business models." This is a sharp turnaround from the practices firms adopted a decade ago shortly after SOX was passed. Most of the then Big 5 accounting firms divested their consulting businesses, and PwC was no exception.

In October 2002, PwC sold its consultancy business to IBM for approximately $3.9 billion in cash and stock. But beginning in 2009, PwC began to backtrack by acquiring firms—including Paragon Consulting Group and BearingPoint, the North American commercial practice that succeeded KPMG Consulting—to rebuild its consulting practice. PwC continued its acquisition strategy by adding Diamond Management & Technology Consultants Inc. in 2010 and a firm called PRTM in 2011. In 2012, PwC acquired a social media strategy development and consulting firm called Ant's Eye View so that it could augment its growing customer impact and customer engagement capabilities in management consulting. The 2013 acquisition of Booz & Co. was a natural follow-on.

Ernst & Young (EY) coped with divesting from its consulting practice by selling it to Capgemini SA, a large global consulting firm headquartered in Paris, France. EY isn't known to have engaged in large-scale merger activity after 2002, when it acquired some of the remaining practices of Arthur Andersen outside the United States. Its French website doesn't mention providing consulting services, but its U.S. website indicates that the firm provides advisory services related to performance improvement, performance technology, and risk.

The smallest of the Big 4, KPMG, spun off its consulting practice in 2000 as KPMG Consulting. The company went public in 2001 and was renamed BearingPoint a year later. It fell on hard times, and its U.S. operations declared bankruptcy in 2009. It sold major segments of its global practice, including selling North American Public Services to Deloitte and North American Commercial to PwC.

Deloitte, which is competing with PwC to be the largest accounting firm, is the only one that didn't divest its consulting practice after SOX was enacted. Its consulting website calls it the largest consulting firm in the world, providing perhaps the most diverse array of consulting services. General categories of the consulting services it provides include analytics, business transformation, digital enterprise, human capital, strategy and operations, technology services, and innovation. Additional services are provided under the heading Financial Advisory Services and Deloitte Growth Enterprise Services.

In addition to part of BearingPoint, Deloitte also acquired Drivers Jonas in the United Kingdom in 2010, plus ClearCarbon Consulting and DOMANI Sustainability Consulting in 2011 to augment its offerings in the field of sustainability. Deloitte entered the mobile application field in 2012 when it acquired Übermind, Inc. and Monitor Group after Monitor filed for bankruptcy.

There are many potential dangers to the independent auditing function as the Big 4 accounting firms (and undoubtedly many smaller firms) become preoccupied with consulting services, and the PCAOB has started to take notice. In a December 2013 speech at the American Institute of Certified Public Accountants (AICPA) National Conference on SEC and PCAOB Developments, the PCAOB's Doty posed a number of questions dealing with the impact of consulting on audit quality:

- "Of what consequence are these developments for the audit function? What are the implications for independence of the audit function?"
- "What will firm management do to meet the compensation and cultural challenges that destabilized Arthur Andersen?"

- "How will firms avoid talent misallocation, with the best minds going to consulting at the expense of audit expertise and competence?"
- "What is the capability of audit leadership to evaluate and manage other business lines away from audit?"
- "What are the risks of other business lines and how do they affect resource allocation and investment in audit?"

Doty also noted that "audit firms have said that the acquisition and ownership of nonaudit expertise benefits and supports audit expertise." Following his speech, however, he questioned that assertion, wondering about the extent to which firm consulting expertise can impact audit quality and auditor performance. The personnel who perform audit services are different from those who perform consulting services. The logic of the benefits to auditing has never been clearly explained to the public user.

In the midst of this, public reports on audit quality continue to be disappointing. In April 2014, the International Forum of Independent Audit Regulators (IFIAR) released a global survey of audits conducted by the six largest audit firms. Titled "Report on 2013 Survey of Inspection Findings," the survey "indicates the persistence of deficiencies in important aspects of audits and that there is a basis for ongoing concerns with audit quality."

In the 1930s, to serve the public interest, Congress mandated that all public companies engage independent auditors to perform periodic auditing services. Many of these audit providers have merged over time, which means the vast majority of these services are now provided by only a very few firms. Economists characterize this situation as an oligopoly. A 2012 academic study, "The Capture of Government Regulators by the Big 4 Accounting Firms: Some Evidence," found that regulators "have failed to indict any of the Big 4 for known criminal actions" because of a "too concentrated to indict" modification of the "too big to fail" doctrine.

The public interest isn't being served if we stand by while accounting firms become global, giant, broad-scope financial service enterprises designed to serve a wide variety of the needs of client management with a lesser commitment to perform the highest-quality independent audits. It's hard to see how such firms can effectively serve the conflicting interests of such disparate groups of stakeholders. Firm management attention and resources inevitably follow the business line providing the greatest profitability. But we can't permit the consulting excesses and "please-the-client" culture that led to the demise of Arthur Andersen and collapse of Enron to occur ever again.

Can Truly Independent Auditors Be Co-opted?

The Defense Contract Audit Agency (DCAA) plays a critical role in protecting the interests of taxpayers by monitoring financial aspects of federal defense procurement contracts and subcontracts. The DCAA provides auditing, accounting, and financial advisory services in connection with negotiation, administration, and settlement of contracts and subcontracts to the Department of Defense (DOD) and other federal agencies. These services must comply with generally accepted government auditing standards (GAGAS) promulgated by the U.S. Government Accountability Office (GAO). The standards provide guidance to auditors performing government audits and other reviews to maintain competence, integrity, objectivity, and independence.

On July 22, 2008, the GAO issued a disturbing report, *DCAA Audits: Allegations that Certain Audits at Three Locations Did Not Meet Professional Standards Were Substantiated,* that illustrates how the objectivity of auditors, who are expected to function on a truly independent basis, can be co-opted by pressures from the contractor and DOD contracting community as well as other factors. Whistleblower complaints on the GAO's FraudNet hotline triggered investigations of 14 DCAA audits and forward-pricing audit issues in three California DCAA field offices. The GAO review involved more than 100 interviews and included cooperation with the DOD Office of Inspector General and its Defense Criminal Investigative Service. The DCAA audits in question were issued from 2003 to 2007.

Founded in 1965, the DCAA is under the overall authority, direction, and control of the Under Secretary of Defense (Comptroller and Chief Financial Officer), who is one of only five Under Secretaries reporting directly to the Secretary of Defense. The Under Secretary of Defense (Acquisition, Technology, and Logistics) oversees the Defense Contract Management Agency (DCMA), which actually administers contracts relating to the DOD acquisition system, research and development, installation management, military construction, procurement, and more. This high-level reporting relationship should provide sufficient independence for auditors of the DCAA to report effectively on any ethical missteps.

Unfortunately for taxpayers, ethical transgressions in defense contracting have been with us for decades. The Packard Commission was created more than 20 years ago to develop solutions to continuing scandals that had eroded public confidence in the defense industry, including reported instances of waste, fraud, and abuse within both the industry and the DOD. One of the Packard Commission's major recommendations was to improve the industry environment and public confidence by placing greater emphasis on self-governance. The Commission's January 1986 report notes:

"To assure that their houses are in order, defense contractors must promulgate and vigilantly enforce codes of ethics that address the unique problems and procedure incident to defense procurement. They must also develop and implement internal controls to monitor these codes of ethics and sensitive aspects of contract compliance."

The Defense Industry Initiative on Business Ethics and Conduct (DII), a voluntary organization consisting of virtually all of the major defense contractors, was organized later in 1986 to coordinate and facilitate these efforts. This organization continues to function today (www.dii.org), requiring annual certification of a signatory company's compliance with the DII's six principles of business ethics and conduct: **1.** Each company will have and adhere to a written code of business ethics and conduct. **2.** A company's code establishes the high values expected of its employees and the standard by which they must judge their own conduct and that of their organization; each company will train its employees concerning their personal responsibilities under the code. **3.** Each company will create a free and open atmosphere that allows and encourages employees to report violations of its code without fear of retribution for such reporting. **4.** Each company has the obligation to self-govern by monitoring compliance with federal procurement laws and adopting procedures for voluntary disclosure of violations of federal procurement laws and corrective actions taken. **5.** Each company has a responsibility to each of the other companies in the industry to live by standards of conduct that preserve the integrity of the defense industry. **6.** Each company must have public accountability for its commitment to these principles. The DCAA appears to use many quality and ethical control strategies. In addition to supervisory and other reviews, methods include the independence standards of GAGAS, reliance on contractor ethics initiatives, and the mandatory requirements contained in the Truth in Negotiations Act. All seemed ineffective in the audits reviewed by the GAO in July's report. The allegations of failure to meet standards were all substantiated: (1) Work papers didn't support reported opinions, (2) DCAA supervisors dropped findings and changed audit opinions without adequate audit evidence for their changes, and (3) sufficient audit work wasn't performed to support audit opinions and conclusions. Seven contractors were involved, two of which are among the top five in terms of contract value.

One of the most glaring examples of a lack of independence cited in the GAO report was the finding of collusion. The GAO found that "contractor officials and the DOD contracting community improperly influenced the audit scope, conclusions, and opinions of some audits—a serious independence issue." In other words, there was an upfront agreement between the resident auditor and contractor executives regarding which records would be selected for audit and the decision that the audit opinion would be based on final and corrected documents after several DCAA reviews. Even after all this advance effort, there was sufficient evidence to support a determination of systems inadequacy.

When the contractor objected to the draft findings at the exit conference, the DCAA resident auditor replaced the original supervisor and senior auditor and threatened personnel action if the senior auditor didn't change the work papers and draft opinion. According to the senior auditor, whom GAO interviewed, he initially refused to make the changes but later did so after being pressured by the resident auditor, who didn't want the report to differ from other recent opinions. An Air Force official told GAO that he advised the DCAA senior auditor not to "lose his job" over the disagreement and to go ahead and make the necessary changes to the working papers.

Another disturbing finding reported by the GAO is the lack of available experienced staff to complete the analysis of complex cost data required by the Federal Acquisition Regulation (FAR) and other audits. According to DCAA data, planned downsizing has decreased the number of auditors from almost 6,000 in 1989 to about 3,500 in fiscal 2007—despite significant increases in military spending during that period for the Gulf war and Iraq war. Further, the DOD strategy of outsourcing functions previously performed by military personnel increased the proportion of total defense spending allocated to contractors. DCAA auditors told the GAO that the limited number of hours allowed for their audits and the number required to be completed directly affected the sufficiency of audit testing.

Perhaps most disturbing is that the GAO identified a pattern of frequent management actions that served to intimidate the auditors being interviewed and to create an abusive environment. In this environment, some auditors "were hesitant to speak to [the GAO] even on a confidential basis." An ethical culture in the organization is critical to the proper functioning of controls.

According to a July 23, 2008, press release from Senators Joseph Lieberman (I.D.-Conn.) and Susan Collins (R.-Maine), the two Senate

addressees of the GAO report, mismanagement of federal contracts is one of the biggest operational challenges facing the federal government. The two Senators coauthored comprehensive legislation, passed by the Senate, to address the weak oversight and lack of competition in contracting. The website of the report's House of Representatives addressee, Henry Waxman (D.-Calif.), didn't contain any information about his reaction to the GAO findings.

There are several lessons to be learned from this situation. The first is that even a very comprehensive control system may be unable to assure successful outcomes if those charged with oversight—in this case, Congress—fail to perform their function effectively and on a timely basis. The GAO refers to a January 2007 report, *High-Risk Series: An Update*, which states, "[The] DOD is not able to assure that it is using sound business practices to acquire the goods and services required to meet the needs of U.S. warfighters." The phrase "high risk" in the report's title refers to a greater vulnerability to fraud, waste, abuse, and mismanagement.

The second lesson is that cost-pinching reductions in resources devoted to auditing efforts may have counterproductive results. Although the current report notes that noncompliance with GAGAS has had an unknown effect on the government, "downsizing of contract oversight staff in the 1990s coupled with hundreds of billions of dollars in increased contract spending since 2000 has exacerbated the risks associated with DOD contract management." Perhaps the cost-saving business model of stationing a resident auditor at many contractor locations provides too much of an opportunity for auditors to become familiar with contractors, resulting in loss of independence.

The DCAA website notes that there are 300 field audit offices (FAO) and suboffices located throughout the United States and overseas. An FAO is identified as either a branch office or a resident office. Suboffices are established by regional directors as extensions of FAOs when required to furnish contract audit service more economically. With so many auditors based in such close proximity to their audit clients, employing traveling auditors assigned to audit multiple contractors is possibly the only way auditors can function with independence. This structure would prevent auditors from having constant contact with the same set of contractor executives and military officers and would provide a base removed from all contractor organizations, where independence can be regularly reinforced.

The third lesson to be learned is the importance of regularly reinforcing an ethical culture. The federal government provides considerable guidance for achieving ethical success. Beyond GAGAS, available governmental guidance includes the work of the DOD Standards of Conduct Office and the U.S. Office of Ethics. Despite these efforts, however, the DCAA seems to need a much more vibrant ethical culture to sustain sufficient independence to perform its mission. Ethics is a matter of the heart and not just legal rules of the head.

Hypothetical Earnings Trigger Real Bonus Payments

The Revenue Reconciliation Act of 1993 caps the deductibility of executive salaries at $1 million, but bonus payments of any amount are deductible if they result from the achievement of established performance goals. Many public companies today take advantage of the performance-based bonus payment system, using misleading bonus calculations to give "superior performance" bonuses at the expense of shareowners and taxpayers.

The congressional Joint Committee on Taxation reports that these tax-advantaged bonuses cost the U.S. Treasury $3.5 billion per year. Dozens of corporations reward subpar returns to shareowners. According to the September 13, 2013, *Bloomberg News* article, "Companies Use IRS to Raise Bonuses With Earnings Goals," the CEOs of 63 large companies in the Standard & Poor's (S&P) 500 Index received cash bonuses in 2012 based on corporate performance even though their company's shares underperformed that of the Index. *Bloomberg* quotes Robert Reich, the secretary of labor under President Bill Clinton, who said, "Taxpayers are losing billions of dollars; shareholders are being taken for a ride."

Tax-deductible bonuses based on company performance were undoubtedly allowed because Congress believed it's in the best interests of shareowners: Performance-based compensation includes stock option and appreciation rights awards. At least two outside independent directors must approve the performance goals, and a majority of shareowners must approve the incentive compensation program. The company's compensation committee—composed of external, independent directors—must certify that the appropriate goals have actually been met.

Unfortunately for taxpayers and many shareowners, "any company can define performance 'more or less as it chooses,'" according to Michael Doran, a lawyer who served in the Treasury Department's Office of Tax Policy under Presidents Clinton and George W. Bush. Now a law professor, Doran believes the IRS rules have "merely served to undermine the concept of 'performance.'" He continued, "Failure can be treated as success for purposes of exemption."

The cause of this divergence of the financial results reported to shareowners and those used for bonus purposes appears to be a growing emphasis on financial measures that aren't audited or based on Generally Accepted Accounting Principles (GAAP). In addition to utilizing non-GAAP measures for the calculation of bonuses, many companies provide analysts and investors with public information adjusted by management to exclude nonrecurring and other various items.

A search of the ProQuest database in May and June 2013 found more than 6,000 news articles and wire releases that contained non-GAAP information while announcing corporate earnings for the first quarter, giving a revenue outlook or earnings guidance for the year, or providing other information for investors and analysts.

In addition to the fact that non-GAAP financial information isn't audited, another difficulty with its use is that there are no accounting principles to guide its preparation. Thus the information may be subject to manipulation. Consequently, non-GAAP financial measures presented by a company may differ substantially over time and lack comparability with similar information from other companies, even when the same terms are used to identify the measures. Companies also may make unannounced adjustments to non-GAAP earnings in order to meet bonus targets or analysts' expectations.

Consider, for example, Exelon Corp., a New York-based nuclear energy company. The Exelon board of directors added $85 million ($0.06 per share), which the company never actually earned, to the 2012 audited earnings report. This boosted the "performance" of the company enough so that top executives could receive tax-deductible bonuses.

To its credit, Exelon painstakingly provided considerable information on how unaudited, non-GAAP financial measures were used to calculate its executive incentive performance awards. Its 2013 Proxy Statement provides 45 pages of disclosures mandated by the Securities & Exchange Commission (SEC) concerning matters affecting compensation. Yet how many shareholders are able to fully comprehend this content?

The Statement defines compensation as salary, annual incentive plan, nonqualified stock options, performance share unit awards, and restricted stock unit awards. Additional elements of compensation include pension, supplemental pension, savings plan, deferred compensation plan, and perquisites. It also describes the three guiding principles of Exelon's compensation program:

1. Link compensation to performance results,
2. Align the interests of its named executive officers and shareholders,
3. Provide competitive compensation opportunities.

The Proxy Statement further notes: "A majority of executive compensation is performance-based and is tied to our financial and operational performance, individual performance and Exelon stock price performance." Yet even though former Exelon CEO John Rowe's incentive bonuses grew nearly 49% between 2007 and 2011, Exelon shareowners haven't fared well, according to *Bloomberg's* analysis. The company's operating profits and market value have fallen by half in the past five years. During that period, executives still received bonuses for above-target performance in four of the five years, amounting to more than $20 million. In a February 7, 2013, press release, Exelon announced it was reducing its annual dividend on common shares from a rate of $2.10 to $1.24 per share.

The influence of tax deductibility on Exelon compensation is also set forth in its Proxy Statement: "The compensation committee's policy has been to seek to cause executive incentive compensation to qualify as 'performance-based' in order to preserve its deductibility for federal income tax purposes to the extent possible, without sacrificing flexibility in designing appropriate compensation programs." It also notes that "despite the challenging operating environment, the company closed the year within adjusted earnings guidance."

Exelon's Statement presented its 2012 audited earnings per share (EPS), based on GAAP, as $1.42. To arrive at the publicly reported, adjusted non-GAAP operating EPS of $2.85, management made 10 adjustments that amounted to a net increase of $1.43 per share, a little more than 100%. (The non-GAAP results were also included in the February press release and discussed in Exelon's earnings conference call on the same date.)

Adjustments that increased non-GAAP EPS included plant retirements and divestitures ($0.29), merger and integration costs ($0.31), Maryland commitments related to merger ($0.28), amortization of commodity contract intangibles ($0.93), and Federal Energy Regulatory Commission (FERC) settlement ($0.21). These adjustments increased EPS by $2.02.

The adjustments that decreased non-GAAP EPS included mark-to-market impact of economic hedging activities ($0.38), unrealized gains related to nuclear decommissioning trust funds ($0.07), and

reassessment of state deferred income taxes ($0.14). Their total effect was a decrease of EPS by $0.59.

But that's not all. The EPS that was used for bonus purposes was $2.91. The additional $0.06 per share of non-GAAP earnings (approximately $85 million) the board of directors added is described in the Proxy Statement as "Adjustment by Compensation Committee." The rationale for this action, according to Gary Prescott, the company's vice president of compensation, was to offset unexpected rate decisions by Illinois regulators that cut actual earnings. The Statement noted that "the outcome of these deliberations was not known at the beginning of the year when the budget was established."

Other companies seem to use significant discretion in setting performance goals for deductible bonus purposes and determining if they have been achieved. According to *Bloomberg,* Las Vegas-based gaming company Wynn Resorts Ltd. uses earnings before interest, taxes, depreciation, and amortization (EBITDA), a non-GAAP measure. For CEO Steve Wynn, the goal he needed to achieve to receive a full bonus was set at a level lower than prior-year results in both 2011 and 2012. Wynn easily exceeded the targets and collected tax-deductible bonuses of $9.1 million in 2011 and $10 million in 2012.

Another example of questionable logic is the case of CEO Scott Boruff of Miller Energy Resources, an oil and gas exploration company. For Boruff to earn his performance bonus, the company had to achieve "a higher percentage increase" in common stock return than its peers. Miller's shares actually fell by 5.9% during the year, but the board of directors decided to award a $1 million performance bonus to Boruff anyway, saying he had achieved a "lower percentage decrease" than competitors.

Yet another tactic that a number of companies employ, according to *Bloomberg,* is to set a non-GAAP EPS goal that's substantially lower than analysts' expectations—even though most analysts rely heavily on a company's guidance and outlook for the future. For example, Valero Energy set its bonus earnings goals for 2011 and 2012 "at least 37% below analysts' consensus estimates" of actual performance. This practice makes it easy to support the $3.7 million in incentive payments for CEO Bill Klesse each year.

Let's hope that companies will do the right thing for their shareowners and for taxpayers at large by discontinuing the use of misleading bonus calculations and instead make performance bonuses a reward for actual superior performance. Exelon, for one, employed a new compensation consultant in 2013 and made six substantive changes to its 2013 compensation program. These moves were partially in response to feedback from shareowners, 25% of which voted against the company's program in the 2012 advisory "Say on Pay" vote.

The Pay-for-Performance Misnomer

A new study of Standard & Poor's (S&P) 1,500 companies by the Investor Responsibility Research Center Institute (IRRCi) finds "a major disconnect between corporate operating performance, shareholder value and incentive plans for executives." The IRRCi disseminates research on issues that intersect corporate responsibility and investors' informational needs. Its latest study explains that many of today's senior executives are evaluated on short-term accounting measures and the price of company stock. This obscures consideration of management's contribution to real long-term economic performance so that only 12% of the variance in CEO compensation is explained by performance of the entity.

In addition to the results of the study, I believe the corporate compensation committees of boards of directors and their consultants utilize self-determined non-Generally Accepted Accounting Principles (GAAP) accounting measures and low-ball "performance" goals to ensure payment of incentive compensation to executives regardless of whether the outcome is favorable for shareowners or whether the executive contributed to achieving the outcome.

Study Faults Compensation Methodology

The IRRCi study, "The Alignment Gap Between Creating Value, Performance Measurement, and Long-Term Incentive Design," describes the "overwhelming dependence of large U.S. companies on total shareholder return (TSR) as a dominant performance and incentive compensation metric." The report criticizes this practice because it doesn't recognize the cost of capital and also is subject to many vagaries that have little, if any, relationship to a single company's operating performance and the success of strategic decisions or the influence of executive management and the CEO. Extraneous factors include the level of the flow of federal funds into or out of the stock market, industry influences, commodity prices, and changes in regulatory rules.

One likely cause of the focus on specially defined performance metrics is the cap of $1 million on the deductibility of executive salaries contained in the Revenue Reconciliation Act of 1993. Bonus payments in any amount are deductible if they result from achieving previously established performance goals. Corporate bonuses paid to CEOs—some of the richest

individuals in the country—are being funded by taxpayers. A further incentive to base much of executive bonuses on stock market performance is the tax preference given to capital gains earned in as little as one year. According to the study, overreliance on TSR and short-term accounting metrics distracts attention from the real drivers of economic performance and doesn't sufficiently focus on factors that CEOs actually influence.

Short-term Thinking

An important finding in the study is the preponderance of short-term measurements that are contained in many of the long-term incentive compensation program designs. Only 10% of respondents' executive incentive plan designs define "long term" as three years or more. Nearly a quarter of companies have no long-term performance-based awards, relying instead on stock options and time-based restricted stock in their long-term compensation plans. This converts long-term into medium term at best.

The study found that nearly 60% of the S&P 1,500 changed their performance metrics used in their incentive calculations in 2013, which further reinforces and actually compounds the short-term thinking about "long-term" executive compensation. One-third of the companies changed 25% or more of the list of peer group companies they use for comparison in 2013, losing comparability over time. Despite the ostensible long-term nature of this portion of executive compensation, these actions highlight the short-term focus and desire of board compensation committees and their consultants to pay a tax-deductible bonus despite the reality of corporate economic performance.

Additionally, the research showed that very few companies use a measure of future value in their executive incentive design, which would include measures such as return on innovation, growth, and return from new product development and new markets. Focus on "making the quarterly numbers" in the short term may lead to decisions detrimental to the firm, such as deferring maintenance, curbing research and development projects, or failing to invest in new long-term strategies.

Economic Profit

Perhaps the most critical finding in the IRRCi study is that 75% of the S&P 1,500 companies have no cost of capital metrics or balance sheet data in the design of their long-term incentive plan. The report describes inclusion of this factor as a value-creating fundamental. This omission means that the most common measurement metrics used to evaluate the performance enterprises today and the design of long-term incentives to guide executive decisions don't necessarily align directly with underlying sustainable value creation for shareholders. For an enterprise to be sustainable in the long term, economic profit or economic profit improvement must turn positive before capital and liquidity run out.

Economic profit, consisting of net operating profit after tax (or return on invested capital, ROIC) minus a charge for capital, is an enhanced and more effective value-creation performance measure because it takes into account the amount of invested capital as part of measuring overall value creation. It also facilitates thinking about sustainable value creation because it can be used to split a company's market enterprise value into current and future value. Only about 17% of companies specifically disclose the use of ROIC or economic profit as a determinant of long-term performance in their plan for setting the long-term portion of executive compensation. Today, more than 85% of the S&P 1,500 have no disclosed "line of sight" leading or process metrics in their proxy statements that are aligned to future value, innovation, and related drivers.

Based on their TSR and economic profit for the years 2008 to 2012, the S&P 1,500 companies can be split into four groups that represent a phase in the value-creating life cycle:

- 35.4% generated both a five-year positive TSR compared with their peers and a five-year positive cumulative economic profit (ROIC exceeding cost of capital). This is a positive sign that represents sustained growth and high performance.

- 17.3% had a positive relative TSR but a negative five-year cumulative economic profit. This is a positive sign that represents early growth or a turnaround.

- 17.9% had a negative relative TSR but a positive cumulative five-year economic profit. This is a negative sign that represents mature growth or harvest.

- 29.4% had negative relative TSR and negative five-year cumulative economic profit. This is a negative sign that represents a restructure or new business model.

Only about one-third of the companies in the S&P 1,500 qualify in the most desirable quadrant, yet generous bonuses seem to be paid to executives regardless of the economic performance of their company.

Actual Bonus Calculations

The final question answered by the research is, "How do companies actually design their compensation programs and calculate their executive bonuses?" Using a 10-year correlation analysis (2003-2012) of 1,200 companies over five-year rolling periods, the five-year geometric average realizable compensation for CEOs is $22 million. Variance from this average can be explained statistically by the following factors:

- Size of revenue, industry, inflation (44% variance);

- Economic performance, e.g., relative TSR five-year ROIC (12.4% variance); and

- Consistent company pay policy (19.2% variance).

The remaining 24.6% is not explained by known factors and could be the result of arbitrary decisions, frequent changes in plan provisions, and the like. A 2013 study from Cornell and McGill Universities, "CEO Bonus: Alternative Performance Versus Gamesmanship," examines the managerial and economic consequences of using non-GAAP performance metrics to set bonuses. It also received a best paper award from the American Real Estate Society. The report has two important conclusions. The first is that "capital market participants also penalize [non-GAAP] manipulations, as firms with larger manipulation have lower market value and higher cost of capital, irrespective of whether these manipulative activities are driven by CEO bonus or other concerns." The second conclusion is that "external regulatory and market oversights are required to ensure fair reporting of non-GAAP information" when non-GAAP performance measures are used aggressively to determine CEO compensation.

Let's hope that more companies will do the right thing by discontinuing the use of misleading or noneconomic bonus calculations and instead make performance bonuses a reward for actual superior, sustainable economic performance.

IMA Ethics Code Compares Favorably to Global Code

The International Federation of Accountants (IFAC) is a global association of professional accountancy bodies from 127 countries. These national organizations represent accountants in public practice, education, governmental service, industry, and commerce. IFAC's mission is to contribute to the development, adoption, and implementation of high-quality international standards and guidance. Ethical guidance is provided by the International Ethics Standards Board for Accountants (IESBA). Its mission is to set high-quality ethical standards for professional accountants and facilitate the convergence of international and national ethical standards, including auditor independence requirements, through the development of a robust, internationally appropriate code of ethics.

The latest codification of the *IESBA Code of Ethics for Professional Accountants* (IESBA Code) was issued in 2009 and published as a handbook in 2010. The IESBA Code is divided into three sections of guidance: (1) general applicability, (2) for professional accountants in public practice, and (3) for professional accountants in business (PAIB). The fundamental principles of general applicability are:

Integrity—to be straightforward and honest in all professional and business relationships.

Objectivity—to not allow bias, conflict of interest, or undue influence of others to override professional or business judgments.

Professional Competence and Due Care—to maintain professional knowledge and skill at the level required to ensure that a client or employer receives competent professional services based on current developments in practice, legislation, and techniques and to act diligently and in accordance with applicable technical and professional standards.

Confidentiality—to respect the confidentiality of information acquired as a result of professional and business relationships and, therefore, not disclose any such information to third parties without proper and specific authority unless there's a legal or professional right or duty to disclose, nor use the information for the personal advantage of the professional accountant or third parties.

Professional Behavior—to comply with relevant laws and regulations and avoid any action that discredits the profession.

In comparison, the *IMA Statement of Ethical Professional Practice* (the *IMA Statement*) contains an unqualified commitment that all IMA® members shall behave ethically. IMA's commitment to ethical professional practice includes overarching principles that express our values and standards that guide our conduct. The overarching principles in the *IMA Statement* are honesty, fairness, objectivity, and responsibility.

The fundamental principles portion of the IESBA Code also provides a conceptual framework that all professional accountants shall use to:

- "Identify threats to compliance with the fundamental principles,
- "Evaluate the significance of the identified threats, and
- Apply safeguards, when necessary, to eliminate the threats or reduce them to an acceptable level" (Section 100.2).

Safeguards within organizations designed to protect against threats to compliance with the fundamental principles specifically applicable to PAIBs include:

- "The employing organization's systems of corporate oversight or other oversight structures.
- The employing organization's ethics and conduct programs.
- Recruitment procedures in the employing organization emphasizing the importance of employing high caliber competent staff.
- Strong internal controls.
- Appropriate disciplinary processes.
- Leadership that stresses the importance of ethical behavior and the expectation that employees will act in an ethical manner.
- Policies and procedures to implement and monitor the quality of employee performance.
- Timely communication of the employing organization's policies and procedures, including any changes to them, to all employees and appropriate training and education on such policies and procedures.
- Policies and procedures to empower and encourage employees to communicate to senior levels within the employing organization any ethical issues that concern them without fear of retribution" (Section 300.14).

The IESBA Code describes potential threats someone would face in attempting to comply with the fundamental principles and prescribes related safeguards. The *IMA Statement**, however, provides 13 standards that express concise and detailed requirements for ethical conduct that members of IMA must follow. They are grouped into four categories: Competence, Confidentiality, Integrity, and Credibility.

The portion of the IESBA Code that provides guidance for PAIBs consists of five parts: Potential Conflicts, Preparation and Reporting of Information, Acting with Sufficient Expertise, Financial Interests, and Inducements. An introduction notes that a PAIB, particularly one in a senior position, is expected to encourage within his or her organization an ethics-based culture that emphasizes the importance that senior management places on ethical behavior. According to the IESBA Code, potential conflicts may arise for PAIBs when their responsibilities to their employers clash with their professional responsibilities. Conflicts also may arise because of pressure to act in ways that aren't in accordance with the Code's fundamental principles. Pressure may be explicit or implicit and may come from a supervisor, manager, director, or another individual within the employing organization. A PAIB may face pressure to:

- "Act contrary to law or regulation.
- Act contrary to technical or professional standards.
- Facilitate unethical or illegal earnings management strategies.
- Lie to others or otherwise intentionally mislead (including misleading by remaining silent) others, in particular auditors of the employing organization or regulators.
- Issue or otherwise be associated with a financial or nonfinancial report that materially misrepresents the facts, including statements in connection with, for example: The financial statements, tax compliance, legal compliance, or reports required by securities regulators" (Section 310.3).

The IESBA Code provides examples of safeguards to help protect against such pressures. This includes "Obtaining advice, where appropriate, from within the employing organization, an independent professional advisor or a relevant professional body, using a formal dispute resolution process within the employing organization, [and] seeking legal advice" (Section 310.3).

When discussing the preparation and reporting of information, Section 320.1 of the IESBA Code states that PAIBs "shall prepare or present such information fairly, honestly, and in accordance with relevant professional standards so that the information will be understood in its context." If this isn't possible, PAIBs "shall refuse to be, or remain, associated with information they determine to be misleading" (Section 320.5). If PAIBs discover that they were unknowingly associated with misleading information, they must take steps to be disassociated from that information. In determining whether there is a requirement to report such information, PAIBs may consider obtaining legal advice as well as whether to resign.

In regard to acting with sufficient expertise or performing duties with the appropriate degree of professional competence and due care, the IESBA Code indicates that potential threats could include having:

- "Insufficient time for properly performing or completing the relevant duties.
- Incomplete, restricted or otherwise inadequate information for performing the duties properly.
- Insufficient experience, training and/or education.
- Inadequate resources for the proper performance of the duties" (Section 330.3).

Concerning financial interests, Section 340.3 of the Code requires that PAIBs "shall neither manipulate information nor use confidential information for personal gain." Neither shall PAIBs "offer an inducement to improperly influence professional judgment of a third party" (Section 350.7).

In December 2011, the IESBA proposed new language in the Code that provides more specific guidance for professional accountants to identify, evaluate, and manage conflicts of interest. The changes should help professional accountants to identify a potential conflict of interest earlier and prompt them to better evaluate their ability to be objective and meet the other fundamental principles contained in the Code. Specifically, PAIBs are tasked to be alert to interests and relationships that a reasonable and informed third party would be likely to conclude might compromise compliance with the fundamental principles.

The proposal also expands the section of the IESBA Code concerning financial interests to include the topics of compensation and incentives linked to financial reporting and decision making. Many of the examples of self-interest threats describe situations highlighting the link between reported earnings and triggers for bonus payments and grants of stock options.

The *IMA Statement* is more clear and concise and thus likely to give more helpful guidance in that several paragraphs are devoted to detailed suggestions of the courses of action that IMA members should consider in identifying unethical behavior or resolving an ethical conflict. These are contained in the section titled "Resolution of Ethical Conflict." The approach contained in the IESBA Code is that PAIBs should evaluate the significance of potential threats to unethical behavior against the safeguards designed to prevent such behavior. This requires the individual to come to a personal decision without specifying actions to achieve this goal. The *IMA Statement* is superior in that it clearly and concisely sets forth behavioral standards that management accountants should follow and action steps they should take.

Provision of specific guidance to help management accountants apply the overarching principles and behavioral standards contained in the *IMA Statement* is likely to be more effective and lead to more ethical behavior than the approach taken by the IESBA Code.

*The *IMA Statement* was revised after this column was published and is available at www.imanet.org/career-resources/ethics-center?ssopc=1. The revision requires IMA members to actively contribute to a positive ethical culture.

IFAC Updates Code of Ethics

One of the missions of the International Federation of Accountants® (IFAC®), a "global organization for the accountancy profession dedicated to serving the public interest by strengthening the profession and contributing to the development of strong international economies," is to contribute to the development of global high-quality standards and guidance in various areas of accounting. The IFAC group that performs this task in the area of ethics is the International Ethics Standards Board for Accountants® (IESBA®).

The IESBA's mission is to set "high-quality ethics standards for professional accountants" and work toward convergence of global and national standards. According to IESBA's 2013 Annual Report, *Reinforcing Trust in the Profession,* issued November 19, 2014, this mission contributes "to public confidence in the accounting profession." The report's publication was delayed following the passing of IESBA Chair Jörgen Holmquist in March 2014, thus it includes developments and actions from both 2013 and 2014.

In his introduction to the report, Wui San Kwok, interim chair of the IESBA, writes, "Ethics is the foundation on which public trust in the accounting profession is built." Consequently, the most important IESBA strategy to continue to reinforce public trust is to promote the recognition and widespread adoption of the *IESBA Code of Ethics for Professional Accountants* throughout the world. Outreach to stakeholders continues to be an important activity that is undertaken by Board members and IESBA staff. To ensure that the Code remains relevant in the face of new developments in the accounting world, the Board established an Emerging Issues and Outreach Committee.

Final and Potential Changes to the Code

In March 2013, the IESBA published *Changes to the Code of Ethics for Professional Accountants Addressing Conflicts of Interest,* a final pronouncement that provides more comprehensive guidance of situations that could possibly involve a conflict of interest. This revision to the Code, which became effective July 1, 2014, is equally applicable to professional accountants in business and in public practice. It's helpful in identifying, evaluating, and managing circumstances that might involve conflicts of interest.

Perhaps the most controversial and challenging topic facing the Board is determining the best way to provide guidance on whether professional accountants should overturn their ethical responsibility to confidentiality when faced with circumstances that can be considered noncompliance with laws and regulations. To address this issue, the Board published an exposure draft, *Responding to a Suspected Illegal Act,* in 2012. The draft resulted in more than 70 comment letters, so the IESBA sponsored three global roundtables of stakeholders in 2014. In its January 2015 meeting, the Board approved the key objectives for accountants in its new Proposed Response Framework.

On a related topic, on May 20, 2014, the IESBA published an exposure draft that deals with the ethical ramifications of independent auditors providing nonassurance services to audit clients. Fifty-nine comment letters were received in response. The exposure draft, *Proposed Changes to Certain Provisions of the Code Addressing Non-Assurance Services for Audit Clients,* covers only certain portions of the Code relating to this subject, namely clarifying management's responsibilities. IMA's Committee on Ethics issued a comment letter advocating significant revisions to the exposure draft, including expanding its scope to cover more aspects of providing nonassurance services to audit clients. At its January meeting, the Board unanimously approved updates relating to the withdrawal of emergency acceptance provisions, management responsibilities, and clarifications about how to prepare accounting records using mechanical services.

Implementing the Code Worldwide

IFAC includes more than 175-member organizations in 130 countries, encompassing 2.5 million accountants in public practice, education, government service, industry, and commerce. With a group that broad and varied, an IESBA working group was tasked to determine ways to improve the usability of the Code, thereby facilitating its adoption, effective implementation, and consistent application around the world.

The working group recommended clarifying and simplifying the language contained in the Code, highlighting actual requirements for compliance, and developing an electronic Code. In October 2014, the Board requested comments from stakeholders on possible approaches to the Code that could improve its clarity and usability by revising its structure. IMA's Committee on Ethics plans to respond to this request. Then in December 2014, the Board launched a web-based version of the Code designed to provide enhanced access and greater ease of use and navigation.

The Board also has chosen to focus considerable attention on Part C of the Code, which applies specifically to professional accountants in business (PAIB). Phase I of this project consists of an exposure draft, *Proposed Changes to Part C of the Code Addressing Presentation of Information and Pressure to Breach the Fundamental Principles.* (Phase II will deal with inducements.) The proposed changes in Phase I include:

- "Fuller and more explicit guidance regarding PAIBs' responsibilities when presenting information;

- Strengthened guidance on how a PAIB can disassociate from misleading information;

- An expanded description of pressure that may lead to a breach of the fundamental principles in the Code together with practical examples to illustrate different kinds of situations in which such pressure may arise; and

- New guidance to assist PAIBs in identifying and responding to pressure that could result in a breach of the fundamental principles."

IESBA Technical Director Ken Siong says, "The development of this enhanced guidance reflects a rebalancing of the board's focus to be more inclusive of PAIBs, a very large and important part of the accountancy profession." IMA's Committee on Ethics plans to submit advocacy comments concerning both phases.

Since 2013, IMA has been a full member of IFAC and is one of only two organizations in the group based in the United States. IMA members must comply with the *IMA Statement of Ethical Professional Practice,* which the Committee on Ethics is tasked to assure its contents continue to be no less stringent than those in the IESBA's Code.

Fraud Continues, but So Does Good Corporate Citizenship

Conventional wisdom indicates that a recession results in more fraud being committed. In fact, the 2009-2010 edition of the *Kroll Global Fraud Report* found that companies lost an average of $8.8 million to fraud over the past three years, an increase of 7% over last year's average. Hardest hit were financial services firms—more than 90% reported being a victim of some kind of fraud. The findings result from a global survey of more than 700 senior executives in diverse industries performed by the Economist Intelligence Unit.

According to Kroll President Tim Whipple, "What goes up [in a recession] is the discovery of fraud, not always the same thing [as its commission]." He added, "Just like legitimate businesses, fraudsters are threatened by loss of income or the financial weakness of their businesses; Ponzi schemes are especially vulnerable. But other fraudulent areas—management conflict of interest, corruption, employee theft—also come to light when business conditions sour."

The Kroll report goes on to describe industry and regional trends and to explain details of its findings. While the recession has increased the motivation to commit fraud, at the same time, less business activity provides reduced opportunities for corrupt practices. Three factors that often increased vulnerability to fraud in the past are having less effect this year: high staff turnover, entries into new and unknown markets, and interfirm collaboration. In the down economy, these factors have mostly decreased in many companies. Lower profits do heighten other risks, however, such as reduction in staff devoted to internal controls in order to save money. One in six respondents to the survey saw this vulnerability increase from last year's results.

In industry terms, the Kroll report states that the financial services sector, with broad and deep exposure to many risks, saw its average fraud loss climb to $15.2 million, an 18% increase. The sector has the greatest opportunities for fraudulent behavior. Fraud risks include money laundering, financial mismanagement, regulatory and compliance shortfalls, internal financial fraud, and loss or theft of information. The handling of other people's money in so many circumstances requires healthy controls and other antifraud measures, including staff background checks and formal risk management systems run by high-level risk officers.

In comparison, the average fraud in the construction, engineering, and infrastructure industry dropped by more than half to $6.4 million. Its fraud issues are largely related to its risk profile, caused by the nature of its contracts and operations as well as its supply chain. In construction, as well as a number of other industries, the year also saw a marked increase in the levels of corruption and bribery, reflecting the greater importance of governmental contracting.

At the economy-wide level, the contrasting tendencies almost cancelled each other out. A cautionary message expressed by the Kroll report is that when the current economic situation turns more positive, the fraud risk kaleidoscope will take another turn, with different issues and exposures. Each industry needs to continually prioritize the threats it faces and then establish the measures it is ready to take to detect, prevent, or mitigate those threats.

The report notes that companies, especially those in financial services, would be well advised to adopt the following fraud risk mitigation strategies:

- Robust employee screening;
- Data security from both internal and external threats;
- Transaction monitoring for anomalies that may indicate money laundering, corruption, or other fraud;
- Facilities through which employees can report all suspicions of wrongdoing—anonymously, if required—and the capacity to investigate resulting information independently of the business areas involved;
- Appropriate due diligence on customers and suppliers;
- Staff training in all areas of fraud prevention, particularly for senior management that set the tone for the organization.

Fraud Continues, but So Does Good Corporate Citizenship

The continued presence of fraudulently suspicious activities in financial institutions is mirrored in the latest report of the Treasury Department's Financial Crimes Enforcement Network. This agency periodically reports a number of characteristics of the many Suspicious Activity Report (SAR) forms that are filed with it by various segments of the financial services industry. The agency's latest report shows that, in spite of a 27% decrease in filings by money service businesses (perhaps due to a reduction in sending funds to a foreign location), SARs for nondepository institutions as a whole were down only slightly. Further, SAR filings by depository institutions were up by 13%, largely because of increases in mortgage loan fraud. Some of the suspicious activities noted include transactions being conducted in bursts of activity within a short period of time, especially in previously dormant accounts, and unusual mixed deposits of money orders, third-party checks, payroll checks, etc., into a business account.

On a more positive note, the Boston College Center for Corporate Citizenship research study, *2009 State of Corporate Citizenship in the United States,* reports that commitments to corporate citizenship continued despite the recession. Subtitled *Weathering the Storm,* the findings of the study are based on 756 responses from senior executives in a nationally representative sample of small, medium, and large U.S. companies. Previous studies were conducted in 2003, 2005, and 2007. The earlier studies showed that company executives viewed good corporate citizenship as a fundamental part of doing business, but they often allowed aspirations to outpace actions.

Key issues explored by the survey include:

- What changes in corporate citizenship practices are businesses making during these turbulent times?
- What do they see as the best ways to solve the current economic crisis and create a more stable American economy?
- What do businesses see as the most important areas of corporate citizenship in these organizations?
- What motivates companies to be better "corporate citizens," and has this changed since the 2007 survey?
- How well are they incorporating corporate citizenship in their products and services?
- Has their support for the communities in which they operate changed?
- Have they continued to support lower-income or economically distressed communities?
- With whom are they partnering to solve social and environmental problems, and why?

The findings in the 2009 study reveal that companies generally continued their commitment to corporate citizenship despite the recession. Approximately 54% of respondents believe corporate citizenship is even more important in a recession. The top-three areas of good citizenship continue to be: operating with ethical business practices (91% implementing), treating employees well (81%), and managing and reporting company finances accurately (76%). Only 38% of responding companies reduced their philanthropy and giving, and 83% of large companies supported their employees' volunteer efforts in the community. Employment practices encouraging a balance of work and life were backed by 60% compared to 46% in 2007.

Other findings from the *State of Corporate Citizenship* report were that a citizenship gap appeared between the practices of large and small companies. Large companies more or less kept on track with most corporate citizenship efforts during these difficult times, though many did lay off employees. On the other hand, small firms stayed committed to their priority of treating employees well by avoiding layoffs, but they significantly decreased emphasis on other aspects of good citizenship.

The importance of the business value of corporate citizenship was emphasized by the fact that 70% of responding executives (82% from large firms) identified reputation as the No. 1 driver of the strategy. The CEO leads the corporate citizenship agenda in three out of four companies. The breadth of the citizenship commitment is exemplified by the reported finding that environmental sustainability is seen as a major business driver. Sustainable products and services are offered by 52% of all companies and 65% of large companies. In 45% of companies, employees were compensated for ideas that benefited both the bottom line and the environment or community. This compares to 37% in 2007.

Since all of the good citizenship activities contained in the survey are self-reported by senior executives, we have to contemplate whether they do in fact fairly represent the human resource and other policies actually being practiced in the respondents' companies. While it appears that responsibility and sustainability reporting is increasingly viewed as necessary by U.S. companies, the total lack of any independent verification or assurance in such reports is remarkable. Although sustainability reporting standards do exist, there's wide variation in how they're applied. Both accountants and auditors still have a lot of work to do to be sure that all stakeholders receive accurate, complete, and unbiased nonfinancial and financial information.

Penalties for Fraud Are Insufficient to Deter Wrongdoing

The Securities & Exchange Commission (SEC) Annual Financial Report for fiscal 2013 shows that total penalties and disgorgement ordered totaled $3.4 billion, an increase from the prior fiscal year. According to SEC Chair Mary Jo White, the SEC's "robust enforcement program" is aggressive and creative and will continue to focus on financial statement and accounting fraud. Despite these positive assertions, SEC penalties don't seem to be sufficient to deter future wrongdoing.

In a recent egregious case, investors of Diamond Foods, Inc., suffered significant losses because of the deliberate falsification of quarterly and annual results at the company. "Diamond Foods misled investors on Main Street to believe that the company was consistently beating earnings estimates on Wall Street," said Jina Choi, director of the SEC's San Francisco, Calif., regional office. "Corporate officers cannot manipulate fiscal numbers to create a false impression of consistent earnings growth." Despite these strong words, the SEC assessed a penalty of only $5 million against Diamond, which is listed on NASDAQ with fiscal year 2013 revenues of $864 million.

Management's rationale for engaging in the accounting scandal was the perceived absolute necessity to continue to beat Wall Street estimates. In April 2011, Diamond management decided to acquire the Pringles brand from Procter & Gamble and needed to maintain its strong earnings performance in order to pull off the acquisition. The company had previously seen earnings increase from $0.53 per share in 2007 to $1.42 in 2009.

Before going public in 2005, Diamond was predominantly a cooperative of walnut growers. Its most important business and accounting issue each year dealt with the walnut price paid to growers, which easily provided the most feasible means to falsify earnings. The fiscal 2011 10-K annual report to the SEC stated a critical accounting policy:

"We have entered into long-term Walnut Purchase Agreements with growers, under which they deliver their entire walnut crop to us during the Fall harvest season and we determine the minimum price for this inventory by March 31, or later, of the following calendar year. The

final price is determined no later than the end of the Company's fiscal year. This purchase price will be a price determined by us in good faith, taking into account market conditions, crop size, quality, and nut varieties, among other relevant factors. Since the ultimate price to be paid will be determined subsequent to receiving the walnut crop, we must make an estimate of [final] price for interim financial statements. Those estimates may subsequently change and the effect of the change could be significant."

Diamond allegedly managed quarterly and yearly earnings by shifting part of the cost of walnut sales to later periods, thus enabling it to report a strong performance in 2010 and 2011. Its 2011 10-K annual report to the SEC, filed on September 15, 2011, shows diluted per share earnings of $2.22 and $1.36 for fiscal 2011 and 2010, respectively.

On October 3, 2011, Diamond announced that it had "made a pre-harvest momentum payment [$80 million] to walnut growers in early September, prior to the delivery of the fall walnut crop to reflect the fiscal 2012 projected market environment. The payment is accounted for in fiscal 2012 cost of goods sold and is reflected in the guidance provided by the company on September 15, 2011." The stock price peaked on September 20, 2011, closing at $92.47, up from $28.20 on July 31, 2009. An October 27, 2011, special stockholders' meeting approved the Pringles acquisition.

But bad news was on the horizon as growers were confused by the payments they received. On November 1, 2011, a Diamond press release announced a delay in the Pringles closing. The audit committee had decided to initiate an internal investigation because it received "an external communication regarding Diamond's accounting for certain crop payments to walnut growers." The stock price closed on November 7 at $39.09, a drop of 57.7% from the peak. A later press release reported the employment of an independent Big 4 audit firm and a law firm for assistance in conducting the investigation.

On February 14, 2012, the audit committee announced that it had substantially completed its investigation and that Diamond's fiscal 2011 and 2010 financial statements and accompanying independent auditor reports should no longer be relied on. Two new audit committee members were appointed in March 2012, and in April the company reported the termination of its previous agreement with Procter & Gamble to acquire the Pringles business.

Because Diamond wasn't able to report quarterly financial results for fiscal 2012 following its release of 2011 results, it requested forbearance against delisting from NASDAQ. It finally amended its annual report on Form 10-K in November 2012 with restated results for fiscal years 2011 and 2010. The amounts of reductions in earnings were significant, as were the narrative descriptions of material weaknesses in internal control that allowed the misstatements.

Instead of diluted earnings per share (EPS) of $2.22 for 2011 as originally reported, the restated amount was only $1.17, a reduction of nearly half. For 2010, restated EPS was $0.82 compared to $1.36 originally reported, a reduction of nearly 40%. The closing stock price the day after the announcement was $15.36, a whopping 83% decline from its peak just more than a year earlier.

While the correction of walnut cost accounted for the majority of the difference (reductions of 101% in 2011 and 117% in 2010), there were other corrections as well, including previously unrecognized and unrecorded accounts payable and accrued expenses, such as advertising, and other corrections related to stock-based compensation, foreign currency translation, timing of prepaid and expense recognition, capital lease designation, and deferred income tax. Apparently all of these corrections were considered to be immaterial—individually and in total—when the original financial statements were prepared.

The report of the independent audit firm contained in the 2012 annual report on Form 10-K to the SEC issued just days later contains additional insight as to the causes of the fraud. It notes three material weaknesses in internal control that still existed as of July 31, 2012:

- **Control environment:** "Management's operation style and concentrated decision making increased the risk of management override of certain controls, limited effective communication and flow of information throughout the organization and to those charged with governance and did not provide an environment that consistently encouraged open discussion of alternate views or opinions."

- **Walnut grower accounting:** "The material weakness in the control environment contributed to material weaknesses in walnut grower accounting control activities."

- **Accounts payable and accrued expenses:** "The controls over recording accounts payable and accrued expenses were improperly designed and were not operating effectively to ensure that all expenditures were identified and recorded in the appropriate account and period." (In other words, the accounting was very sloppy.)

The two individuals allegedly involved in this mess are then CFO Steven M. Neil, whose total fiscal 2011 compensation was $2.4 million, and then CEO Michael J. Mendes, whose total fiscal 2011 compensation was $7.3 million. Both were placed on administrative leave in early 2012 and resigned a month later.

The settlement with the SEC, announced in January 2014, didn't even involve an admission of guilt. The almost trifling $5 million penalty seems to be more like a slap on the wrist than an amount designed to deter future wrongdoing by others. More importantly, shareowners not only have lost much of their investment, but they have also been burdened with more than $200 million in costs related to acquisitions and integration, settlement of a securities class action lawsuit, audit committee investigation, restatement-related expenses, legal investigation expenses, consulting fees, accrued contract termination expenses, and retention and severance accruals. This is according to the non-GAAP (Generally Accepted Accounting Principles) analysis contained in the September 30, 2013, earnings press release.

The SEC also reported settling with Mendes, who should have known that Diamond's reported walnut cost was incorrect at the time he certified the company's financial statements. He paid a minimal penalty of $125,000 but didn't admit or deny the fraud charges. His attorney says Mendes is focusing on new opportunities in his professional career. The SEC should have barred Mendes from ever again serving as an officer or director of a public corporation.

The SEC's litigation continues against Neil, who is fighting the fraud charges and looks forward to trial. His attorney says he has done nothing wrong: "He followed long-standing company practice and an accounting treatment that was approved by the company's outside auditors." Stakeholders in the investment community deserve a verdict that provides appropriate penalty for Neil's unethical and fraudulent behavior that will deter future wrongdoing by others.

Did Ernst & Young Really Assist Financial Fraud?

After nearly two years of wondering where the auditors were during the financial meltdown, New York State Governor Andrew M. Cuomo has finally provided some possible answers regarding the activities of the auditing firm for the now bankrupt Lehman Brothers. In September 2008, Lehman's bankruptcy represented the largest filing in U.S. history and resulted in an immediate 500-point drop in the Dow-Jones Industrial Average. This previously highly prominent global financial services giant was one of the few Wall Street firms allowed to trade directly with the Federal Reserve System, and the group's members continue to be considered the most influential and powerful nongovernmental institutions in world financial markets.

When he was New York's attorney general, Cuomo filed a lawsuit in late December 2010 in the New York Supreme Court claiming that Ernst & Young (E&Y), a Big 4 firm, helped hide Lehman's "fraudulent financial reporting." These acts were alleged to have occurred during a seven-year period leading up to the Lehman bankruptcy. What Lehman did and E&Y allegedly specifically approved was to consider some borrowing, done under agreements to later repurchase the notes, as a sale of an asset rather than a short-term borrowing arrangement.

According to the attorney general's complaint, E&Y "substantially assisted Lehman to engage in a massive accounting fraud, involving the surreptitious removal of tens of billions of dollars of securities from its balance sheet." The complaint alleges this created a false impression of Lehman's better liquidity, thereby defrauding the investing public and violating New York law.

"This practice was a house-of-cards business model designed to hide billions in liabilities in the years before Lehman collapsed," Cuomo said. He added, "Just as troubling, a global accounting firm tasked with auditing Lehman's financial statements helped hide this crucial information from the investing public."

The specific mechanism used by Lehman and asserted to be approved by E&Y was to engage in what became known as Repo 105 transactions. These deals involved a transfer of liquid fixed income securities by Lehman to European counterparties for cash with the binding obligation they would be repurchased a few days or weeks later. The volume of Repo 105 transactions increased dramatically at the end of each calendar quarter.

Contrary to the usual practice of accounting for repurchase agreements, or "repos," as short-term loans, Lehman characterized Repo 105 transactions as a sale of assets. By using the cash obtained from these "asset sales" at quarter- or year-end to pay down other debts, Lehman reduced the amount of total liabilities it reported and improved its reported leverage ratios and balance sheet metrics. The firm rapidly accelerated its use of Repo 105 transactions in 2007 and early 2008 as the financial crisis grew and Lehman was facing demands to reduce its leverage.

To date, the Securities & Exchange Commission (SEC) has neither taken any regulatory action against Lehman and its officers nor has it accused E&Y of violating any federal rules of accounting or auditing. The SEC did propose new rules on September 17, 2010, requiring public companies to provide increased information in both qualitative and quantitative terms about their short-term borrowings, including those having repurchase obligations. If adopted, these disclosures would be required in the Management's Discussion and Analysis (MD&A) section of their reports to the SEC. According to SEC Chair Mary Schapiro, "misleading 'window dressing' in quarterly reports" was one obstacle to investor confidence.

Did Ernst & Young Really Assist Financial Fraud?

A report issued in March 2010 by Lehman bankruptcy examiner Anton Valukas faults E&Y as well as Lehman senior executives. The report states that Lehman's financial statements were "materially misleading" and that executives engaged in "actionable balance sheet manipulation." The report also cites whistleblowers who attempted to correct what they viewed as improper behavior. Valukas believes that "there is sufficient evidence to support a colorable claim" that certain Lehman officers breached their fiduciary duties and that E&Y was professionally negligent.

In a March 2010 letter to its clients, E&Y defended its audit work for Lehman. The letter states that Lehman's bankruptcy resulted from unprecedented adverse events in the financial markets, declining asset values, and loss of market confidence that caused a collapse in its liquidity. The firm believes the bankruptcy wasn't caused by accounting or disclosure issues, as Lehman's financial statements clearly portrayed it as "a leveraged entity operating in a risky and volatile industry."

One possible justification for treating repo transactions as sales is contained in the infamous derivatives rule, Statement of Financial Accounting Standards (SFAS) No. 140, "Accounting for Transfers and Servicing of Financial Assets and Extinguishments of Liabilities."

This lengthy document discusses the need for the transferor of securities to relinquish all control of securities in order to consider the transaction a sale. If the transferor receives collateral to secure the transaction at less than 102% of the amount transferred, then SFAS No. 140 concludes no real sale has taken place. In its transactions, Lehman believed the additional 3% that made the total collateralization 105%—hence the term "Repo 105"—demonstrated excess collateral and thus resulted in a true sale of securities in spite of the binding obligation to repurchase.

SFAS No. 140 also calls for disclosure of the nature of any repurchase agreement transactions and the amounts and classification of collateral. But this requirement lacks specificity and led to later revisions to SFAS No. 140 and the very recent SEC requirement noted earlier. Lehman had footnote disclosure of off-balance-sheet commitments of almost $1 trillion, excluding the amount of Repo 105 liabilities, but no clear disclosure of the extent of repo transactions. In fact, the complaint filed by then Attorney General Cuomo asserts that Lehman reported that all of its repurchase agreements were treated as financing arrangements, not as sales.

Another obstacle to calling Repo 105 transactions true sales is the fact that apparently Lehman was unable to get any U.S. law firm to provide a legal opinion that they were in fact true sales. A U.K. law firm did provide such an opinion but added the requirement that it be applied only to U.K. repo instruments. Yet Lehman didn't limit its application of the true sale doctrine to the U.K. Instead, the firm used one of its British subsidiaries to put very significant amounts of U.S. securities into the repo pool. Apparently E&Y didn't object to this stretch of circumstances.

The most telling assertion in the complaint concerning E&Y's alleged misrepresentation of Lehman's compliance with applicable accounting standards is that E&Y didn't require the financial statements to reflect economic substance rather than just legal form. In other words, the complaint accuses E&Y of letting Lehman engage in transactions without business purpose in order to achieve a specific financial statement result. This is similar to assertions made in the Enron case—that the auditor, Arthur Andersen, enriched itself by coaching Enron how best to structure transactions so they could remain off its balance sheet. An interesting aspect of the substance-over-form requirement is that it is contained in the auditing standards, specifically AU §411.06, not the accounting literature promulgated by the Financial Accounting Standards Board (FASB).

As accounting standards setters work to converge international and U.S. pronouncements, little attention seems to be directed toward global convergence of audit standards. In the U.K., auditor opinions specifically state that the client's financial statements do in fact present a true and fair view, whereas U.S. audit standards only opine that statements are presented in accordance with U.S. Generally Accepted Accounting Principles (GAAP). It would seem that E&Y would have had more difficulty in expressing a U.K.-type opinion on Lehman.

In summary, the ethical challenges faced by E&Y in deciding how to address issues with a longstanding and profitable client may be faced by many public accountants. In fact, accountants in all areas of the profession frequently face similar ethical issues of simultaneously complying with their duties for faithful service and loyalty to their employer or client while respecting their responsibilities to other stakeholders. "Doing the right thing" for all concerned may sometimes be an impossible assignment. Guidance such as the overarching principles of honesty, fairness, objectivity, and responsibility contained in the *IMA Statement of Ethical Professional Practice* will go a long way toward helping all accountants to do the right thing.

Doing the right thing is always the best policy in the long run.

Toshiba's Toxic Culture

Corporate frauds and ethics scandals aren't limited to companies in the United States. Over the last two decades, for instance, Japan has experienced its share of large financial reporting scandals that have occurred despite laws designed to protect investors and the public. This year, Toshiba Corporation became the latest example.

Misleading Financials

The story unfolded in February 2015 when Japan's Securities and Exchange Surveillance Commission investigated accounting irregularities related to Toshiba's profit recognition on large long-term projects in the areas of nuclear, hydroelectric, and wind-powered equipment; air-traffic control; and other systems. Accounting principles require operational management to estimate the "percentage of completion" that a long-term project has achieved and recognize in each accounting period the current proportionate share of the estimated total profit the project will earn. If a project is forecasted to have a loss, the total amount of the loss must be recognized immediately. This gives management considerable discretion when determining how much progress a project has made at a particular date.

In Toshiba's case, the truthful interim and year-end profit estimates were said to be "too embarrassing" to report to senior management and the public. So the cover-up began during the fiscal crisis in 2008 when Toshiba's president at the time, Atsutoshi Nishida, delivered the ultimatum: "Get it done like your life depends on it." The improper practices continued under the next two company leaders, Norio Sasaki and Hisao Tanaka.

A July 2015 report by an independent investigation committee led by a former top prosecutor and aided by outside lawyers and accountants cited Toshiba's toxic ethical tone at the top as the major cause of its improper accounting practices. The report disclosed inflated profits of at least $1.2 billion and said, "There was a corporate culture at Toshiba under which it was impossible to go against the intentions of superiors." The amount of the fraud was three times the initial estimate.

The July report also said executives put intense pressure on the company's business units to achieve unrealistic profit targets: "Management sometimes issued such challenges shortly before the end of a fiscal quarter or year, encouraging division heads to cook the books." The report noted, "The improper accounting procedures were continuously carried out as a de facto policy of the management, and it was impossible for anyone to go against the intention amid Toshiba's corporate culture."

Another method Toshiba used to manufacture profits was to sell personal computer parts to manufacturers in Taiwan at a higher price than Toshiba had paid for them. The intention initially was to disguise the real costs of its own laptop computers from competitors, but the higher costs were somehow carried over and hidden from quarter to quarter for years.

Poor Oversight

The governance structure at Toshiba was also less than optimal. At the time of the scandal, only four of the 16 board members and nonexecutives were considered outsiders. Because of executives resigning, the board reached a low point of only eight members in 2015, including the same outside directors—two former diplomats, one former banker, and a university professor.

The audit committee, a key factor in effective financial reporting, contained the four outside directors, whose average length of service was approximately two years. The audit committee chair was also a member of the nominations and compensation committees, illustrating the limited number of independent board voices. A new board of directors, of which seven are considered outsiders, was elected at an Extraordinary General Meeting of Shareholders on September 30, 2015.

Experts on Japan cite the weak influence of outside directors and the extensive power that many former CEOs exercise. In *Examining Japan's Lost Decades,* contributing author Kazuhiko Toyama explained, "The biggest cause that ruins Japanese companies is governance led by former executives." There was also a public rivalry at Toshiba between the builder of Toshiba's personal computer business and the long-time head of nuclear power projects. The rivalry split the company into two factions, and neither faction wanted to be looked upon as the cause of the company's difficulties.

After repeated delays, Toshiba reported on September 7, 2015, that its final earnings overstatement for the six-year period amounted to $1.9 billion, nearly 40% of the previously reported income before tax. The company did promise reform, expressing its sincere apology to all of its stakeholders for "any concern or inconvenience." A Management Revitalization Committee, which is composed of outside directors and experts, has been appointed for "comprehensive discussions of measures to prevent any recurrence of accounting irregularities." Recurrence prevention measures encompass reforming the corporate culture, measures for strengthening internal control, and business process reform.

The Outcome

Besides the management resignations, there seem to be few repercussions for Toshiba so far—except that its stock market value saw a steep decline of more than one-third in the six months after the accounting irregularities were first disclosed.

Let's hope that lessons learned from the Toshiba accounting scandal will reinforce efforts to strengthen the ethical culture in many corporations around the world.

The Volkswagen Problem

Following the General Motors (GM) fraud scandal, the revelations that Volkswagen (VW) had installed software on certain cars to cheat emissions testing was yet another example showing the failures of a corporate ethical culture to manage risks properly and limit damage to the company. While the scandals share some similarities, there is a significant difference between the two: Owners of GM cars involved in the recall for ignition switch problems eagerly awaited the opportunity to have a safety violation repaired. VW car owners, however, may not care about a "fix" that will reduce fuel efficiency to minimize pollution.

The VW scandal is an almost unbelievable story. With 12 different brands, Volkswagen AG Group is the largest auto manufacturer in Europe and Germany's largest company with 2014 revenue of €202.4 billion. The Group Management Report portion of the company's 2014 Annual Report touts its superior governance by noting that "transparent and responsible corporate governance takes the highest priority in our daily work." The report claims, "Our pursuit of innovation and perfection and our responsible approach will help to make us the world's leading automaker by 2018—both economically and ecologically (emphasis added)." The Sustainable Value Enhancement Section states, "We run our business responsibly and with a long-term perspective along the entire value chain. Everyone should benefit from this—our customers, our employees, the environment and society."

In 2013, VW said, "We consider responsible and transparent corporate governance to be a key prerequisite for sustainably increasing the Company's value. It helps strengthen the trust of our customers and investors in our work and meet the steadily increasing demand for information from national and international stakeholders." Sadly, these assertions seem to be totally false.

Europe's car makers have worked hard to change the image of diesel autos from their stinky, smoky, and sluggish past. Successful political efforts in Europe have resulted in lower emission standards than in the United States as well as incentives to protect the auto industry, such as generous subsidies to diesel in the form of tax breaks for diesel-guzzling company cars and low duties on the fuel.

VW's strategy aimed to convince customers and regulators that new diesel technology represented the ideal solution to maximize fuel economy and performance while carefully protecting the environment from pollution. VW's German engineering prowess was put to the test but succeeded only by cheating on emissions testing and threatening the health of many citizens of the world, particularly of children and those suffering from respiratory disease. According to *Newsweek*, "Intense ambition and a rigid corporate culture created the conditions for lying."

VW's handling of the pollution issue has caused immense concern among its owners, dealers, investors, employees, and citizens around the world. It wasn't EPA regulatory vigor that exposed the VW lies, nor did VW confess it was breaking the pollution rules. Actually, it was a small research group that was looking for research evidence that U.S. diesels actually were cleaner than those in Europe, where standards are lower. The 2014 U.S. tests showed that VW cars passed in the lab but had significantly higher emissions when driven on the road.

It took some time and a lot of pressure before VW finally admitted its products were faulty and endangering the health of millions around the world. After months of discussions between VW and the U.S. Environmental Protection Agency (EPA), the company admitted the results were due to a "technical glitch" and issued a voluntary recall in December 2014 for nearly 500,000 diesel cars that VW attributed to "various technical issues." When emissions didn't change in 2015, California air quality regulators and the EPA withheld approval for selling any 2016 diesel models, extending the deadline to provide a plan to repair affected vehicles to January 2016, but California regulators rejected VW's plan as "too vague."

Contrary to earlier VW indications that only the two-liter or smaller engines were fitted with a defeat device, the EPA—not VW—discovered that larger three-liter engines, including luxury Audi and Porsche models, also had emission falsification devices. "These latest EPA allegations compound the company's guilt and provide further evidence as to the lack of corporate governance at VW," wrote Evercore ISI analyst Arndt Ellinghorst. He added, "This raises concerns around reporting, transparency and integrity within VW."

To date, VW's actions to deal with the crisis include the almost immediate resignation of CEO Martin Winterkorn, the suspension of employees, and an offer of a "goodwill package" to affected U.S. diesel owners. VW also hired claims attorney Ken Feinberg in November 2015. Feinberg is known for his work on damage suits filed against BP for its Gulf oil spill, GM for its ignition switch issue, and for many September 11 damages.

I don't envy the job Feinberg has: determining how much monetary damage each of the various groups suffered. That involves answering questions like: How should the decrease in value of a car with lower fuel economy be measured? Should it be market-based or calculated based on increased fuel cost? How important is the age of the car? What will motivate owners to get their cars altered? How should citizens be compensated for the health risks to which they have been subjected? Should medical conditions of respiratory disease be factored in? Should California or China receive special consideration because of the smog potential? What did PricewaterhouseCoopers know about the situation?

The most difficult question is: What is an adequate penalty for officers, directors, and employees, as well as the company itself, to assure remediation and no repetition of unethical behavior that has adversely affected millions in many countries?

Small Company Suffers Massive Embezzlements

Koss Corporation is a relatively small, reasonably profitable, and mostly family-owned company with about a quarter of its shares listed on NASDAQ (ticker symbol: KOSS). The almost unbelievable story that continues to unfold around this Milwaukee-based company is that an employee used a large number of unauthorized transactions to embezzle mindboggling amounts of money from her employer. The fraud exceeded the reported earnings in some years at a cost to the company of $31.5 million over five years. This case provides ethical lessons of value to all organizations.

Sujata "Sue" Sachdeva, Koss's trusted, long-serving vice president of Finance, corporate secretary, and principal accounting officer, faces a six-count indictment accusing her of wire fraud for embezzling money for a lavish lifestyle and extravagant shopping sprees.

The sequence of events was rapid. American Express blew the whistle on the scheme because of the huge transfers from Koss's bank to pay Sachdeva's credit card bills. Within days, on December 21, 2009, trading in KOSS on NASDAQ was halted as the company reported the unauthorized transactions. Sachdeva was terminated on December 23, 2009. On December 24, 2009, the Koss audit committee published word that the financial statements for 2006, 2007, 2008, 2009, and first quarter of 2010 "should no longer be relied upon." Baker Tilly Virchow Krause was appointed as the new independent audit firm on January 5, 2010, and on January 11, 2010, Koss's stock resumed trading on the NASDAQ, with the price plunging 24%. On January 18, 2010, Koss announced the hiring of a new executive vice president, CFO, and principal accounting officer.

A Koss Securities & Exchange Commission (SEC) filing made on January 11, 2010, showed preliminary estimates of the amounts of the unauthorized transactions (see Table 1).

According to wire service reports, the indictment alleges that Sachdeva authorized numerous wire transfers of funds from bank accounts maintained by Koss to pay for her American Express credit card bills. In addition, Sachdeva used money from Koss's bank accounts to fund numerous cashier's checks, which she also used to pay for clothing, furs, purses, shoes, jewelry, automobiles, china,

statues, household furnishings, travel expenses for herself and others, renovations and improvements to her home, and to compensate individuals providing personal services to her and her family. She faces a maximum penalty of up to 120 years in prison and fines of up to $1.5 million, plus restitution.

Table 1. Preliminary Estimates of the Unauthorized Transactions

DATE	UNAUTH. TRANS.	EARNINGS BEFORE TAX	PERCENT
FY 2005	$2.2 million	$7.4. million	29.7%
FY 2006	$2.2 million	$10.2 million	22.2%
FY 2007	$3.2 million	$8.3 million	37.9%
FY 2008	$5.0 million	$7.4 million	30.0%
FY 2009	$8.5 million	$2.9 million	293.9%
1st Qtr 2010	$5.3 million	$900,000	574.7%
2nd Qtr 2010	$4.9 million	Not yet released	

Failure to regularly instill new thinking and perspective into the board governance structure as well as the resulting complacency of board meetings has long been considered a likely factor for enabling fraud to occur within a company, and the long tenures of Koss's board members suggest that this might have been a contributing factor to the apparent breakdown of board oversight to detect the large-scale fraud that occurred. The Koss proxy statement for the 2009 annual meeting of shareholders shows that the board met four times during the year. Two of the six board members have the name Koss. Except for a relative newcomer elected to the board in 2006, the length of service for the remaining five averaged 32 years. Excluding founder

John Koss from the calculation, the average length of service was more than 27 years.

The 2009 proxy statement reported that the audit committee consisted of all four non-Koss board members and met three times during fiscal 2009. The chair, who has been a director since 1987, is the president of a holding company established for the purpose of acquiring established companies involved in distributing products to industrial and commercial markets. The designated financial expert on the committee is the retired president of a manufacturer and seller of portable household appliances. In relating the background of committee members, the proxy statement includes no mention of specialized accounting or financial experience.

It appears that the audit committee may have relied heavily on the internal control work of Grant Thornton, according to the committee's report contained in the proxy statement. The report notes that the committee "meets twice a year with the Company's independent accountants to discuss the results of their examinations, their evaluations of the Company's internal controls, and the overall quality of the Company's financial reporting." This report also states that the audit committee "oversees the audit work performed by the Company's internal accounting staff," hinting that there may have been an internal auditing function.

Grant Thornton has somewhat disputed the conclusion that it was involved in evaluation of Koss's internal controls. In the January/February *CFO Magazine*, a spokesperson for the firm says that Koss "did not engage Grant Thornton to conduct an audit or evaluation of internal controls over financial reporting." Audit fees paid to Grant Thornton were $151,000 in 2009 and $71,000 in 2008. Fees amounting to $97,000 in 2009 and $118,000 in 2008 were paid to PricewaterhouseCoopers for tax compliance, tax advice, and tax planning services.

Koss's 2009 Annual Report on Form 10-K contained various assertions that Koss "maintains a system of internal control to provide reasonable assurance that assets are safeguarded and that the books and records reflect the authorized transactions of the Company." Further assertions are made that management, namely Michael Koss, president, CEO, COO, and CFO, had evaluated internal controls over financial reporting (ICoFR) and believed they were effective. Because of its size, Koss isn't yet subject to the Sarbanes-Oxley Act (SOX) requirement that this control assertion by management be attested to by its independent auditor.

The Koss Code of Conduct, published in 2004, sets forth procedures for employees to follow in reporting misconduct, including that Koss "may" implement a corporate compliance hotline for employee, supplier, and customer use. The Code also notes that "when a report relates to an accounting or auditing issue, the complaint procedures adopted by the Audit Board supersede these provisions." The Audit Board could refer to the audit committee of the board.

The only provision in the audit committee charter published in 2006 dealing with ethics is that the committee should "receive, investigate, and retain complaints regarding accounting, internal accounting controls, and auditing matters, including concerns that employees have about questionable matters." Two accountants were terminated because they failed to report the unauthorized transactions to top management or the audit committee.

In summary, the Koss case provides an excellent example of the dangers of:

- Massive weaknesses in internal controls,
- Poor financial oversight by the board of directors and audit committee,
- An apparently obsolete and ineffective ethics and compliance program,
- The external audit firm misunderstanding or not fulfilling expectations of the senior management and audit committee, and
- Failure to report wrongdoing.

How an Embezzler Stole Millions from a Small Company

New details have emerged on the methods used and the outcomes following the case of 47-year-old convicted embezzler Sujata "Sue" Sachdeva. Sachdeva was the trusted 15-year veteran VP of Finance, secretary, and principal accounting officer of Koss Corporation. During a span of more than five years, she stole nearly half the company's pretax earnings. The scheme was uncovered when American Express noticed her credit card balances were being paid through large wire transfers originating from a company bank account. Koss is the Milwaukee-based, mostly privately held small company that's a prominent global designer and marketer of stereophonic headphones.

Sachdeva's criminal case concluded after she pleaded guilty to embezzling $34 million from her employer, an increase of $2.5 million over earlier estimates. The six felony fraud counts carried a maximum penalty of 120 years in jail, but 15 to 20 years is appropriate under federal sentencing guidelines. Because she cooperated with authorities from the very beginning of their investigation, the judge limited her sentence on November 17, 2010, to 11 years in federal prison plus restitution to Koss of $34 million. Her physician husband filed for divorce after the sentencing hearing. Federal officials have seized most of her assets, including a 2007 Mercedes-Benz, timeshares, jewelry, shoes, furs, and other luxury items—some that were never worn because they were put into storage for lack of space. Sachdeva's attorney claims she has a bipolar disease of compulsive shopping disorder and is an alcoholic.

Countering the defendant's plea for a lenient sentence because of mental illness, Koss CEO Michael Koss asked the judge to sentence Sachdeva to the maximum 15 to 20 years, writing that she "stole from the hardworking employees of the company and their families, and ultimately the stockholders of the company." In a presentencing letter, he stated, "The full extent of the damage to the reputation of the company and its employees caused by Ms. Sachdeva's criminal acts cannot be expressed in words." He added that the damage will continue to tarnish Koss and subject it to ridicule long after her sentence ends.

In addition to Sachdeva, the Securities & Exchange Commission (SEC) has charged Julie Mulvaney, former Koss senior accountant, with assisting Sachdeva to conceal the theft on Koss's financial statements by overstating assets, expenses, and cost of sales and by understating liabilities and sales. The SEC accuses both of them in a civil case of maintaining fraudulent records so that Koss filed materially false current, quarterly, and annual reports with the Commission over a period of years. The theft was accomplished through a variety of means, including fraudulent cashier's checks, fraudulent wire transfers, and unauthorized payments from petty cash. A third person, Tracy Malone, a Koss accountant who was fired because she knew about the theft but said nothing, hasn't been charged.

The SEC's August 30, 2010, complaint provides details of the means used by Mulvaney and Sachdeva to get cash by circumventing the internal controls of the corporation. Sachdeva admitted stealing $15 million by authorizing issuance of more than 500 cashier's checks to pay her personal expenses. Cashier's checks were issued directly to retailers, such as Nieman Marcus and Saks Fifth Avenue, and other vendors. Sometimes acronyms were used, like N-M and S.F.A. In addition to using cashier's checks, Sachdeva fraudulently authorized and directed numerous wire transfers, including wiring company funds to American Express to pay for personal purchases on her credit card. From 2008 through December 2009, Sachdeva fraudulently authorized more than 200 bank wire transfers totaling more than $16 million to American Express.

Other methods of fraudulently misappropriating cash for personal use described in the SEC complaint include misuse of petty cash. Sachdeva issued checks payable to "petty cash," had Koss employees then negotiate and return the money to her, which she then used to pay personal expenses. Sachdeva also converted unused traveler's checks that the company had purchased for use by its employees travelling on company-related business and fraudulently used them for herself.

It appears that Mulvaney didn't receive any of the benefits of the massive embezzlements, and she hasn't been charged with theft. But she did materially participate in the cover-up of the fraud and was therefore charged with civil fraud. According to the SEC complaint, the pair were able to hide the huge amounts of missing cash by means of top-side general journal entries. Mulvaney maintained a "red book" containing numerous false journal entries to the company's accounting books and records. She wrote the false journal entries in the red book and then entered them in the company's accounting books and records. By means of those entries, Mulvaney purported to adjust or reclassify the amount of company cash without supporting documentation or any legitimate explanation.

The complaint notes that Mulvaney also prepared falsified accounting books and records and maintained them in a series of colored folders, called the "rainbow files." The rainbow files consisted of seven folders covering fiscal years 1995-2000 (green folder), 2004 (orange), 2005 (blue), 2005 (orange), 2006 (blue), 2007 (yellow), and 2008 (green). The rainbow files included more than 100 fraudulent transactions on the company's books and records.

The rainbow files also reflected a scheme to conceal the receipt of funds by the company through a debit/credit wipe (DC Wipe). A DC Wipe made it appear that a certain transaction (e.g., a sale to a customer and the receipt of funds by the company) never took place. For example, in December 2007, Koss received funds totaling more than $100,000 from an overseas customer. Mulvaney falsified the books and records to make it appear that the company never received the funds. In an attempt to avoid detection, she reduced five separate sales accounts by different amounts that collectively totaled the exact amount—instead of reducing a single sales account by the whole amount.

The fraudulent accounting cover-up also involved the company's sales over the internet and at its retail outlet. From fiscal year 2006 through the time the fraud was discovered during the second quarter of fiscal year 2010 (December 2009), Sachdeva and Mulvaney didn't record in Koss's books any sales made over the internet or at the company's retail outlet, totaling $1.8 million.

Although Sachdeva's fate seems settled, at least for several years, no punishment for Mulvaney has been revealed yet. In a November 17, 2010, *Milwaukee Business Journal* article titled "Sachdeva throws Mulvaney under the train," additional details emerged from the sentencing hearing that show Mulvaney's enabling role in the fraud. Apparently, each year Sachdeva would review the company's cash position a few weeks prior to a scheduled visit from Koss's outside auditors, Grant Thornton. She would presume the difference between the cash in the company's bank accounts and the related ledger accounts was because of her theft of company funds. In a panic, Sachdeva would then call Mulvaney into her office and show her the numbers. Mulvaney would respond by saying, "Let me look at everything and get back to you, and don't worry" and then apparently make the journal entries that no one questioned.

There are other unanswered questions, such as how it was possible that Grant Thornton didn't discover such a massive defalcation. Answers may be forthcoming in the lawsuit Koss has filed against the firm in Cook County, Ill. The complaint alleges that "Grant Thornton, the company's auditor, failed to properly perform audits of the company's financial statements and failed to properly assess the company's internal controls, thus allowing the embezzlement to continue and the damage to the company to escalate." Surprisingly, the lawsuit claims specifically that "Grant Thornton repeatedly assured Koss' management and its board that the company's internal controls were effective and that Koss could rely on those same internal controls and Grant Thornton's work."

Koss's attorney, Michael J. Avenatti, said, "Grant Thornton was paid hundreds of thousands of dollars to properly audit the company's financial statements, and they failed miserably. This failure included repeatedly assuring the company and its board that the company's internal controls were effective. A company should be able to rely on its auditors." For its part, the firm has stated it was not engaged to provide a separate opinion on internal controls. Sarbanes-Oxley Section 404(b) doesn't apply to Koss because it is too small.

The many lessons to be learned from this case seem obvious, especially that smaller companies need to be particularly aware of the possibility of fraud.

Comptroller Steals $53 Million from City Funds

Dixon, Ill., is a town of nearly 16,000 located about 100 miles southwest of Chicago. Its major claim to fame has been that it's the boyhood home of President Ronald Reagan. In April 2012, Dixon began to receive national attention again—this time focused on the massive fraud that the city's 59-year-old comptroller, Rita A. Crundwell, is alleged to have achieved almost single-handedly.

A May 1, 2012, federal indictment charges Crundwell with wire fraud and embezzling approximately $53 million from the city of Dixon since 1990. Over a 20-year period, this works out to about $3,300 for every man, woman, and child living in Dixon. If Crundwell is found guilty, this case would represent one of the largest embezzlements of public funds ever perpetrated. The prison time could be as much as 20 years.

Rita Crundwell graduated with honors from Dixon High School in June 1971, having begun her work at City Hall in 1970 as part of a work-study program. Working for the city, Crundwell continued to gain new responsibilities and move up in job titles. She was appointed comptroller in 1983. She also reportedly played first base during the 1980s for the softball team of Clifton Gunderson, Dixon's independent audit firm at the time. She seemed to avoid politics, having no record of voting since 1998, even in city elections.

During the years, Crundwell pursued an interest in breeding and showing horses. She inherited her first farm property from the estate of her mother, who died in 1984, and kept the property after her 1986 divorce. Crundwell built the first horse stables in 1997, although her salary at the city was a modest $20,000. In 2000, she undertook a major expansion to the house, doubling the living space to nearly 3,500 square feet. She also built a nearly 20,000-square-foot horse barn in 2006 on another 88-acre property in the area, which she purchased from Richard A. Humphrey, Sr., a family member.

Crundwell specialized in breeding horses known as quarter horses, which can run extremely fast for short distances. According to David Giuliani, in his article, "Piecing Crundwell Together" (*McClatchy-Tribune Business News,* April 28, 2012), by 2002 Crundwell was "wowing audiences" at the annual world quarter horse championship

and on her way to national fame and prominence. She told the local newspaper at the time, "I just love to do it, but there is also the agony of defeat that goes with it. There's a lot of that, too."

Over the years, Crundwell became "one of the nation's most famous and most successful horse breeders—her ranch has produced 52 world champions," according to Jim Bret Campbell, spokesman for the American Quarter Horse Association (AQHA). "Rita has owned more world champions than anyone else in our industry," Campbell said (Alyssa Anderson, "Small Town's Comptroller Steals $30 million from City's Coffers," *Left Justified,* April 22, 2012). Most people assumed that the success of her horse farms in Wisconsin and Illinois generated the income for Crundwell to maintain her lavish and wealthy lifestyle.

According to the government's indictment, on December 18, 1990, Crundwell opened a bank account in the name of the City of Dixon, listing "RSCDA c/o Rita Crundwell" as the account holder. Between December 1990 and April 2012, Crundwell used her position as comptroller to transfer funds between the various bank accounts maintained by the city. For example, the FBI sworn affidavit states that from September 2011 through February 2012, a total of approximately $2.8 million was received representing Dixon's share of distributions from the state of Illinois. During the same period, the affidavit states that Crundwell transferred $1.8 million into the RSCDA account she controlled. Between September 2011 and March 2012, she withdrew $3.3 million from the account. Of this amount, only $74,274 was related to city operations.

The FBI affidavit also alleges that Crundwell used Dixon funds to pay for her own personal and private business expenses, including horse farming operations, personal credit card payments, real estate, and vehicles. The affidavit identified Crundwell's vehicle purchases that used funds said to be fraudulently obtained from the city, which included a 2009 Liberty Coach Motor Home for $2.1 million, a 2009 Kenworth Tractor Truck for $146,800, a 2009 Freightliner Truck for $140,000, a 2009 Chevrolet Silverado pickup truck for $56,646, and a 2009 Featherlite Horse Trailer for $259,000.

The sworn affidavit also reports a review of documents provided by American Express showing that between January 2007 and March 2012, Crundwell incurred charges of more than $2.5 million on her personal credit card account. Fifth Third Bank records show that all of these charges were paid by online payments with City of Dixon funds. Charges included more than $339,000 for jewelry from various vendors, averaging more than $5,380 per month.

While Crundwell was living it up, Dixon was experiencing fiscal difficulties. City workers, for example, have had no raises in the past three years. Crundwell covered for the missing funds by taking advantage of the well-known fiscal difficulties of the State of Illinois and claiming that the city's hard times were due to nonpayment by the state. While payments from the state were usually late in arriving, they did come.

Crundwell was known as a smart, hands-on executive. She was in charge of picking up the city's mail at the post office, according to the affidavit. One of Crundwell's relatives—who isn't a city employee—performed this task at her direction. Crundwell was out of town frequently because of her horse business, taking an additional 12 weeks of unpaid time in 2011 in addition to the four weeks paid for by the city. She told a horse enthusiasts' publication in 2003 that her coworkers at City Hall had been accommodating, saying, "They are used to me being gone in August, October, and November." She said she carried a portable computer back and forth, giving her access to her city email, and also called City Hall every day.

In spite of not being in her office all the time, she was able to fool a number of mayors, finance commissioners to whom she reported, and other city council members. Jim Dixon, the mayor from the mid-1980s to the early 1990s, said, "She was pretty much in charge…she was the go-to person." And former Finance Commissioner Roy Bridgeman praised her upon his leaving office last year, saying, "She looks after every tax dollar as if it were her own."

It took the sharp eyes of Kathe Swanson, Dixon city clerk, to uncover the fraud in late 2011. Swanson had made a routine request for all bank statements so she could prepare the monthly treasurer's report in Crundwell's absence. She noticed the "secret" account with Crundwell's name and took it to Mayor Jim Burke, who notified the

FBI. Over the years, Crundwell misled the independent audit firm hired to express its opinion on Dixon's financial statements by allegedly creating fictitious invoices purported to be from the State of Illinois to show that the funds she was fraudulently depositing into the RSCDA account were being used for legitimate purposes.

CliftonLarsonAllen, as Clifton Gunderson became known after its January 1, 2012, merger that made it the eighth-largest U.S. accounting firm according to *Accounting Today*, was Dixon's audit firm for many years through fiscal 2005. At that time, it recommended that Samuel S. Card, a CPA from the nearby town of Sterling, Ill., perform the audit. Thereafter, Dixon continued to retain the Clifton Gunderson firm, but only to accomplish a compilation of its financial statements and not to express a professional audit opinion on them.

The city plans to hire a new firm to handle the audit for the fiscal year that ended in April. At its May 8, 2012, meeting, the City Council hired the firm of Wipfli LLP to restate the earlier audits that are believed to be flawed. Headquartered in Milwaukee, Wis., Wipfli is one of the 25 largest U.S. accounting firms and has an office in Dixon.

It's ironic that President Reagan's popular often-quoted saying, "Trust, but verify," should be so relevant in his own hometown so long after his departure.

Has SOX Been Successful?

The Sarbanes-Oxley Act of 2002 (SOX) was enacted following a series of failures involving various functions designed to protect the interests of the investing public. Containing several highly controversial provisions, SOX created a total revision of the regulatory framework for the public accounting and auditing profession and provided guidance for strengthened corporate governance. It was considered to be the most far-reaching legislation affecting public corporations and their independent auditors since the 1930s.

SOX is widely credited for strengthening at least two major areas of investor protection: (1) CEO and CFO responsibility and accountability for all financial disclosures and related controls and (2) increased professionalism and engagement on the part of corporate audit committees. Yet some continue to question its overall value, citing, as an example, its failure to prevent the situations that led to the financial crisis of 2008.

Section 404

One of the most controversial aspects of the Act is Section 404, which requires company management to provide assertions of effective internal control over financial reporting and for the company's independent audit firm to attest to those assertions.

Congress has been repeatedly pressured to ease this requirement, which it did with the Jumpstart Our Business Startups (JOBS) Act, passed by Congress and signed by President Obama on April 5, 2012. The JOBS Act contained a provision that eliminated the SOX Section 404 requirements for organizations that meet the definition of an emerging growth company.

Aside from requiring management's assertions and the auditor's attestation, SOX Section 404 also requires public companies to disclose whether or not they have adopted a code of ethics applicable to their senior financial officers. For companies listed on the New York Stock Exchange (NYSE), this requirement has been expanded to require listed companies to adopt and disclose on its website a code of business conduct and ethics for directors, officers, and employees and to promptly disclose any waivers of the code for directors or executive officers. The NYSE also provides a list of topics that ethics codes should cover. NASDAQ has adopted similar requirements. All these requirements have significantly elevated the visibility of ethics and made a strong ethical culture a best practice for organizations of all sizes and types.

The significance of a strong ethical culture to organizational success has been the subject of many articles in this column. An ethical culture makes it easier to attract the most qualified employees and minimizes the cost of employee turnover and retraining, which results in optimal productivity and higher profitability. The benefits of a strong social, environmental, and ethical reputation also resonate with a growing number of consumers who want to patronize such firms.

Audit Firm Performance

When evaluating the overall effectiveness of SOX, a vital consideration to make is whether the performance of independent auditors has improved over the last 10 years. The importance of auditor performance is seen in the fact that the first subchapter of the Act provides for a body "to oversee the audit of companies that are subject to the securities laws, and related matters, in order to protect the interests of investors and further the public interest in the preparation of informative, accurate, and independent audit reports." Whether the revised oversight structure adequately regulates public company auditors appears to be an open question even after so many years.

Since auditing became a distinct occupation many hundreds of years ago, auditors have functioned largely as self-regulating professionals. Prior to SOX, important decisions regulating the profession were made largely or exclusively by the auditing industry, its firms, and auditors themselves. These included setting the bar for entry into practice, promulgating the auditing and ethical standards that auditors should employ, determining the quality of performance in using those audit standards, determining whether an auditor violated ethical standards, and disciplining those who failed to practice properly.

When SOX was enacted, the practice of public accounting was divided into audits of publicly held companies and all other entities. SOX established the Public Company Accounting Oversight Board (PCAOB), an independent body under the oversight of the U.S. Securities &

Exchange Commission (SEC). The PCAOB was given the mission to set and enforce practice standards for a new class of firms "registered" to audit publicly held companies. Standards for not-for-profit and governmental entities continue to be set by the industry itself.

An annual speech by the PCAOB Chairman has been the only public evaluation of the quality of performance of audit firms. These reports have expressed only general comments, not comprehensive statistics. In 2011, PCAOB Chairman James Doty stated that PCAOB inspectors had reviewed more than 2,800 engagements of the largest audit firms and "discovered and analyzed hundreds of cases involving what they determined to be audit failures." An audit failure is a defined term describing the most serious deviations from proper practice.

In his 2012 report, Doty noted, "Inspections continue to reveal an unacceptable level of deficiencies." He added that audit regulators around the world had "identified a gap between the purpose of the audit and its fulfillment" because of the possibility that "firms' cultures still impliedly encourage auditors to sell services to their audit clients and, if so, legal or illegal, whether such goals undermine the appropriate state of mind for auditors." These generalizations don't instill confidence in the users of professional auditing opinions. The general requirement in SOX that all findings resulting from PCAOB inspections be held confidential hinders any analysis of perhaps the key measure of audit quality: audit failure. Public reports of annual inspections of specific audit firms contain no details of findings on individual clients. This protects the firm in case of actual or threatened litigation. The PCAOB does have the power to "unseal" portions of the confidential information if it finds that subsequent improvement efforts are "unsatisfactory concerning any particular criticism."

An example of a firm providing unrelated nonaudit services that could impair its independence involves Ernst & Young (E&Y) and the U.S. Chamber of Commerce (USCC). A report by E&Y containing macroeconomic estimates of potential future changes in the U.S. economy was sponsored by four industry organizations: the Independent Community Bankers of America, the National Federation of Independent Business, the S Corporation Association, and the USCC. These economic estimates were designed to show the possible detrimental effect on U.S. jobs and investment by allowing the "top tax rates paid by business owners to rise sharply starting January 1 of next year." The results have been widely publicized by some industry and political lobbying groups, including several of the sponsoring organizations, though it isn't mentioned on the USCC website.

E&Y signed USCC's publicly available Form 990 not-for-profit tax return, which leads one to assume that E&Y is USCC's auditor. Yet in SEC Release 33-8183, "expert services unrelated to the audit" is one of the nonaudit services considered likely to impair an accounting firm's independence if provided to an audit client. One could argue then that an engagement designed as an instrument to directly foster the USCC's mission "to advance human progress through an economic, political, and social system based on individual freedom, incentive, opportunity, and responsibility," which the E&Y report appears to be, falls within the scope of services prohibited by SOX for public company audits and is problematic for other clients.

In an unrelated case of audit failure, on February 8, 2012, the PCAOB announced the censure of E&Y and imposed a $2 million penalty for faulty audits of Medici Pharmaceutical Corporation for 2005, 2006, and 2007 financial statements, its largest civil money settlement to date. It also assessed censure sanctions on four E&Y partners for varying time periods. The respondents neither admitted nor denied the PCAOB findings and didn't consent to make the case public.

An analysis of firm performance reported in PCAOB firm inspections appearing in *Between the Numbers* showed a 20% rate of audit failure at E&Y for 2010, more than double the rate in the 2009 inspections. *Compliance Week* reported even higher audit failure rates at other large firms based on 2010 PCAOB inspections: 22% at KPMG, 39% at PricewaterhouseCoopers, and 45% at Deloitte. Presuming the sample of engagements selected by PCAOB inspectors for analysis is reasonably representative of all audit work performed by the firms, these statistics don't engender the confidence necessary for investors to trust the validity of financial information they are receiving.

SOX Enforcement

To be fair, a great deal of the effectiveness of SOX depends on the vigor to which it's enforced. Questions remain as to whether the SEC's and Department of Justice's enforcement of SOX has been sufficient. A July 30 article in *The Wall Street Journal* notes that SOX's "biggest hammer—the threat of jail time for corporate executives who knowingly certify inaccurate financial reports—is going largely unused."

Although SOX has been successful in increasing corporate focus on a strong ethical culture in publicly owned companies, there's room for improvement in audit firm performance as well as the PCAOB's process for assessing and reporting on it.

Complying with the Foreign Corrupt Practices Act

Congress passed the Foreign Corrupt Practices Act (FCPA) 35 years ago to eliminate bribery of foreign officials by U.S. companies trying to obtain business. Over the years, the scope of the law has grown to include any multinational or foreign-based company that does business in the United States, is listed on a U.S. exchange, or sells securities in the U.S.—thus making compliance with the FCPA an important issue for companies around the globe. In November 2012, the Department of Justice (DOJ) and Securities & Exchange Commission (SEC), the two agencies charged with enforcing the statute, released *A Resource Guide to the U.S. Foreign Corrupt Practices Act,* a detailed compilation of information about the Act, including its provisions and practical advice about how the two agencies pursue their enforcement efforts.

According to the DOJ's website, "The *Guide* addresses a wide variety of topics, including who and what is covered by the FCPA's antibribery and accounting provisions; the definition of a 'foreign official'; and what constitute proper and improper gifts, travel, and entertainment expenses." It also differentiates a bribe from a facilitating payment and the nature of an effective corporate compliance program. Although applicable to publicly held companies, its principles provide best practice guidelines for all organizations, including not-for-profit and government organizations.

The *Guide* also explains the different types of civil and criminal resolutions available in the FCPA context—perhaps the first time this has been done anywhere. Hypotheticals, examples of enforcement actions, and summaries of applicable case law and DOJ opinion releases are all used to describe enforcement practices for both the DOJ and SEC. Jonathan Drimmer, vice president and assistant general counsel for Barrick Gold Corporation, summed up the *Guide* for the Deloitte Forensic Center: "Though it has little new substantive information, it is a very helpful document and provides insight into the decision-making process regarding government prosecutions." It appears that the U.S. government plans to continue to pursue prosecution of bribery cases in every country possible.

As the *Guide* notes, "Corruption is a global problem. In the three decades since Congress enacted the FCPA, the extent of corporate bribery has become clearer and its ramifications in a transnational economy starker. Corruption impedes economic growth by diverting public resources from important priorities such as health, education, and infrastructure. It undermines democratic values and public accountability and weakens the rule of law. And it threatens stability and security by facilitating criminal activity within and across borders, such as the illegal trafficking of people, weapons, and drugs. International corruption also undercuts good governance and impedes U.S. efforts to promote freedom and democracy, end poverty, and combat crime and terrorism across the globe." The DOJ has authority for criminal enforcement of the FCPA, and the SEC is responsible for civil enforcement.

The accounting provisions of the FCPA are designed to complement the antibribery provisions by prohibiting "off-the-books" accounting. Investors, creditors, and even company management rely on financial statements and internal controls to ensure reporting transparency about the financial health of the business, the risks undertaken, and the transactions between the company and its customers and business partners. The SEC says that the FCPA's accounting provisions "strengthen the accuracy of the corporate books and records and the reliability of the audit process which constitute the foundations of our system of corporate disclosure."

In a chapter titled "Guiding Principles of Enforcement," the *Guide* describes the differing approaches of the DOJ and SEC in regard to enforcement. For example, guidance to U.S. attorneys in deciding whether to initiate or decline prosecution is contained in the *Principles of Federal Prosecution.* The *Guide* notes that, according to the *Principles of Federal Prosecution,* it will be appropriate in many investigations "for a prosecutor to consider a corporation's pre-indictment conduct, including voluntary disclosure, cooperation, and remediation, in determining whether to seek an indictment."

In contrast, the *Guide* notes how the SEC's *Enforcement Manual* suggests considering such factors as "the statutes or rules potentially violated; the egregiousness of the potential violation; the potential magnitude of the violation; whether the potentially harmed group is particularly vulnerable or at risk; whether the conduct is ongoing; whether the conduct can be investigated efficiently and within the statute of limitations period; and whether other authorities, including federal or state agencies or regulators, might be better suited to investigate the conduct."

In the same chapter on enforcement, the *Guide* also outlines the hallmarks of effective ethics and compliance programs:

1. Commitment from senior management and a clearly articulated policy against corruption;

2. Code of conduct and compliance policies and procedures;

3. Oversight, autonomy, and resources;

4. Risk assessment;

5. Training and continuing advice;

6. Incentives and disciplinary measures;

7. Third-party due diligence and payments;

8. Confidential reporting and internal investigation;

9. Continuous improvement, including periodic testing and review; and

10. Pre-acquisition due diligence and post-acquisition integration for mergers and acquisitions.

The chapter titled "Resolutions" describes possible outcomes to investigations. The DOJ may settle cases through a plea agreement, a deferred prosecution agreement (DPA), or a nonprosecution agreement (NPA). A DPA means that the DOJ files a charging document with the court but simultaneously requests that the prosecution be deferred so that the company can demonstrate its good conduct. DPAs generally include a monetary penalty, waiver of the statute of limitations, full cooperation with the government, and admission of relevant facts. The company also must commit to stated compliance and remediation changes. An NPA isn't filed with a court but is instead held by the parties. According to the *Guide*, the DOJ "maintains the right to file charges but refrains from doing so to allow the company to demonstrate its good conduct during the term of the NPA."

Deloitte's Forensic Center has conducted a number of surveys of FCPA ethics and compliance activities. Its *Anti-corruption Practices Survey 2011* found that only 29% of the executives surveyed were very confident their company's anticorruption program would prevent or detect corrupt activities. A poll during a December 2012 Deloitte webcast showed many companies still have a long way to go in FCPA compliance. In fact, 44.6% of poll respondents said either that their companies aren't making improvements to prevent and detect corrupt

activity or that they are unaware if their company is doing so. "The 55.4% that do have plans to improve their corruption programs are 'in line with the government's expectations,'" says Bill Pollard, a partner in Deloitte's FCPA consulting practice.

In a 2012 publication concerning the DOJ/SEC guidance, *New FCPA Resource Guide: Ten Things for Legal and Compliance Officers to Consider,* Deloitte reported several potential reasons that might inspire a low level of confidence in a company's antibribery program. These reasons suggest 10 areas of ethics and compliance that need attention:

1. The most critical way to defend against FCPA exposure is a preexisting compliance program that is risk-tailored and risk-based.

2. In the eyes of a regulator, the tone at the middle and tone at the bottom of a company will define the effectiveness of the tone at the top.

3. FCPA compliance is the responsibility of a senior executive who must work to ensure adequate staffing and resources.

4. Third-party compliance is essential, must be risk-based, and must include purposeful and intelligently designed auditing and monitoring.

5. Controlled subsidiaries, affiliates, and joint ventures must be taken into account in FCPA compliance.

6. Even noncontrolled affiliates, joint ventures, distributors, and dealers should be included in the risk assessment and compliance plan.

7. Financially immaterial transactions and payments may give rise to material liability, reputational harm, and management distraction.

8. The ultimate test for an FCPA compliance program is "Does it work?" Companies must be prepared to prove that it does.

9. Privately held companies should be on notice that they also have FCPA risk exposure.

10. The U.S. government will continue to apply expansive jurisdictional concepts in order to enforce the provisions of the FCPA globally.

The favorable effects of establishing and maintaining a strong, open, and transparent corporate culture that's based on the highest standards of ethics have long been documented in previous columns. The DOJ's and SEC's focus on the importance of self-reporting and cooperation with federal investigations makes this emphasis even more important, as the government continues to show signs of growing vigilance in enforcing the FCPA. For example, *The Wall Street Journal* reported on March 19, 2013, that federal regulators are investigating Microsoft Corp.'s relationship with business partners that allegedly bribed foreign government officials in return for software contracts. The story advised that the Microsoft investigation is one of "dozens" being conducted under the FCPA.

Fight Against Corruption Escalates

The fruits of a recently announced U.S. Department of Justice (DOJ) initiative to stop foreign corporate bribery resulted in the arrest for bribery of 22 top-level executives in the arms industry. The case was described as the largest prosecution ever of individuals for foreign corporate bribery under the 1977 Foreign Corrupt Practices Act (FCPA). Included in those arrested was the sales vice-president of Smith & Wesson, the largest manufacturer of handguns in the U.S.

Lanny A. Breuer, U.S. assistant attorney general for the criminal division, described the FBI stings that obtained evidence to support the arrests as "the first time we've used the technique of an undercover operation in a case involving foreign corporate bribery." He added, "The message is that we are going to bring all the innovations of our organized crime and drug war cases to the fight against white-collar criminals." Breuer noted, "International cooperation is growing every day and getting better and better."

The most prominent group organized to fight corruption on a global scale is Transparency International (TI). TI's mission is to create change leading to a world free of corruption. It defines corruption as the abuse of entrusted power for private gain. According to TI, corruption hurts everyone whose life, livelihood, or happiness depends on the integrity of people in a position of authority. Perhaps the group's best-known research product is its annual *Corruption Perceptions Index* (CPI), which ranks the perceived level of public-sector corruption in 180 countries and territories around the world as measured by expert and business surveys. In the 2009 report, the United States ranked 19th, a slide down from 14th at the beginning of the decade.

In terms of paying business bribes, the *2008 Bribe Payers Index* report from TI ranks Belgium, Canada, the Netherlands, and Switzerland as the least likely of 30 leading exporting countries to use bribes to win business abroad. Countries rated as most likely to use bribery as a sales tool are China and Russia. The U.S. falls in the middle.

TI's *2009 Global Corruption Barometer* surveyed 673,000 households in 69 countries concerning their perceptions of and experiences with corruption. The report showed that 53% of respondents believe the private sector of business to be corrupt, using bribes to influence public policy, laws, and regulations, up from 45% in 2004. "These results show a public sobered by a financial crisis precipitated by weak regulations and a lack of corporate accountability," said TI Chair Huguette Labelle.

TI also publishes an annual *Progress Report on Enforcement* of the Organisation for Economic Co-operation and Development (OECD) Anti-Bribery Convention. The 2009 document shows that enforcement has been extremely uneven. There's active enforcement in only four countries and little or no enforcement in 21. The *Report* calls for increased efforts in countries with moderate enforcement because their level of enforcement isn't high enough to provide effective deterrence. Many senior executives were totally unaware of the contents of this global document. In November 2009, the OECD published a revised *Recommendation of the Council for Further Combating Bribery of Foreign Public Officials in International Business Transactions*. The United Kingdom introduced a strengthened bribery bill into Parliament in November 2009.

A more positive note is reflected in the TI *Global Corruption Report 2009*. It reveals "encouraging and real progress" toward stronger corporate integrity despite prominent corruption scandals and the "lack of transparency and accountability that has been shown to lie at the root of the financial crisis." But corporate performance in this area often doesn't live up to the commitments made by senior corporate executives. The key message of the *Report* is that "business world-wide now has a clearer responsibility, more profound self-interest and greater potential" to have a vital role in lessening the burden of corruption.

The *Global Corruption Report 2009* sets forth a number of business-related findings and conclusions that point to a need for change:

- Corrupt payments to public officials are only one part of the corruption problem. Nepotism and corruption in private business transactions are two issues that deserve much more attention. Corrupt practices tend to invalidate the license that society grants to business to operate, and they damage the legitimacy and trust that business depends on to survive.

- Corruption within an enterprise is a widespread threat to sustainable performance and accountability. An example is majority business owners who enter into conflicted self-dealing contracts that harm other stakeholders. This type of corruption also hinders companies from acting as good corporate citizens.

- Corruption in the market for goods and services undermines fair competition and prices and results in higher costs globally. There's evidence of a new and potent wave of globalized cartel activity involving well-known brand names and key market sectors, ranging from food and vitamins to the most sophisticated high-tech products and consumer services.

- Corruption risks in corporate lobbying can turn legitimate participation in the democratic decision-making process into undue influence. The 2009 *Report* contains case studies that document a precariously close nexus between private businesses and public institutions. There are real questions of equal visibility and right to be heard by all citizens who can't afford to hire lobbyists.

- Corruption at the individual firm level raises costs and introduces uncertainties and reputational risks. Thus, the business case for fighting corruption is strong—good governance and corporate integrity pay "integrity dividends." Companies with anticorruption programs and ethical guidelines experience up to 50% fewer incidents of corruption.

The *Report* combines these findings and conclusions into a number of policy proposals for corporate action:

1. Report publicly on key aspects of corporate citizenship. While great progress has been made in improving nonfinancial reporting practices, TI believes that additional information about lobbying and political finance activities is necessary so that all stakeholders can understand how corporate interests make their voices heard in the political arena.

2. Make commitments to corporate integrity and codes of conduct more verifiable and their monitoring more transparent. This will enable top-performing companies to lead by example and turn promises into more credible performance.

3. Support existing standards and collective action frameworks. Rather than developing idiosyncratic, self-serving reporting methods, companies should embrace, support, and actively engage in extending existing principles, such as the Global Reporting Initiative. Comparable reporting among similar enterprises greatly enhances transparency.

Similar recommendations are included for governments, regulators, and society as a whole.

Another group involved in fighting corruption is TRACE International, a nonprofit membership association that pools resources to provide antibribery compliance solutions. A press release TRACE issued in 2009 reports evolving trends in FCPA enforcement by the DOJ and the Securities & Exchange Commission (SEC). The trends reported include record levels of enforcement, greater multijurisdictional cooperation, and an increasing focus on the prosecution of individual wrongdoers.

The release describes the Nature's Sunshine Products case where its Brazilian subsidiary paid bribes to customs officials to allow importation of unregistered product. The corporate COO and CFO were convicted of failure to supervise employees with responsibility to maintain accurate books and records and internal controls. It wasn't necessary to show that these executives either knew anything about or participated in the unlawful conduct, only that they held significant decision-making authority.

Principle 10 of the United Nations Global Compact states: "The one who cheats will be cheated against." Even if a company merely tolerates corrupt practices in some situations, that fact will become known—both inside and outside the organization. The Compact continues: "Unethical behavior erodes staff loyalty to the company." It's difficult for employees to understand why high ethical standards should be applied within a company when the same standards don't apply to relations with suppliers and customers. This dichotomy erodes trust and confidence, which are so necessary for effective operations. The lesson for all to learn and continually practice is that ethical behavior is the right thing to do at all times and in all circumstances.

Whistleblowing Reaches Center Stage

Whistleblowing continues to emerge as an important tool in uncovering wrongdoing and prosecuting or punishing offenders. Several recent court cases have been settled successfully based on whistleblowing efforts, and advocacy groups and government regulators in both the United States and the United Kingdom took additional steps toward supporting whistleblowers.

The latest progress comes from the U.S. courts system. In the span of a few weeks, a whistleblower lawsuit filed by a former University of California-Irvine (UCI) professor and anesthesiologist who blew the whistle on illegal practices resulted in an agreement by the California Board of Regents to pay $1.2 million to the United States. In Alaska, an employee was granted a settlement of $3.5 million in a whistleblower retaliation case after suing his former employer for wrongful termination. And in Maine, a security worker was awarded more than $200,000 in damages and attorney fees for wrongful termination in a whistleblowing case.

During this same time, several Texas healthcare companies agreed to pay $2.3 million to settle civil allegations that they engaged in false or fraudulent conduct by double billing the Texas Medicaid program, among others. In Florida, a nonprofit hospital repaid nearly $3 million it received from overbilling the government before the matter came up in federal court. In New York, a former employee of celebrity tailor Mohanbhai Ramchandani will receive a $1.1 million reward for blowing the whistle on Ramchandani for underreporting millions of dollars of income and sales taxes. Stephen A. Weiss, who represented the whistleblower, noted that the "settlement demonstrates how necessary and effective whistleblower laws are in uncovering small business fraud that may be known and visible only to company insiders."

Government agencies and other groups are also making progress in increasing whistleblowing efforts. The Government Accountability Project, a U.S. whistleblower advocacy organization, is engaged in its 2012-2013 American Whistleblower Tour, which visits college campuses and other locations to promote its message of "corporate and government accountability by protecting whistleblowers, advancing occupational free speech, and empowering citizen activists." It uses social media and other means to convey to the public its core message of strengthening whistleblower rights.

The U.S. Securities & Exchange Commission (SEC) released the first full-year report of its Office of the Whistleblower, which was established under the Dodd-Frank Act of 2010. The Office administers an initiative to promote payment of monetary awards and increased protection to individuals providing significant new information helpful in prosecuting large, successful enforcement actions.

The *2012 Annual Report on the Dodd-Frank Whistleblower Program* shows that the agency received and processed 3,001 tips, complaints, and referrals (TCRs) during the 2012 fiscal year. Additionally, in the four months of the year that a telephone hotline was available, the agency received 3,050 calls. The most common subjects of the TCRs were corporate disclosures and financials (18.2%), offering fraud (15.5%), and manipulation (15.2%). An "other" category made up 23.4% of the TCRs.

Of the TCR submissions received, 83.5% were from within the U.S., with the remaining 16.5% coming from other countries, including 3.5% from the U.K., 1.5% from Canada, 1.1% from India, and 0.9% from the People's Republic of China.

"In just its first year, the whistleblower program already has proven to be a valuable tool in helping us ferret out financial fraud," then-SEC Chairman Mary L. Schapiro said in November 2012. "When insiders provide us with high-quality road maps of fraudulent wrongdoing, it reduces the length of time we spend investigating and saves the agency substantial resources."

The SEC's Investor Protection Fund awarded the Commission's first Whistleblower Award Program recipient in 2012, but the case and individual haven't been made public. The Fund represents monetary sanctions received from settlements of SEC cases, including penalties, disgorgement, and interest. The balance at the end of fiscal 2012 was $453 million. In addition to funding the Whistleblower Award Program, the Investor Protection Fund finances the operations of the Inspector General's Employee Suggestion Program.

The SEC's whistleblower report also indicates that "there were 143 enforcement judgments and orders issued during fiscal year 2012 that potentially qualify as eligible for a whistleblower reward." Also, "the Office of the Whistleblower provided the public with notice of these actions because they involved sanctions exceeding the statutory threshold of more than $1 million."

In the United Kingdom, a new independent commission was formed to "make it easier" to raise the alarm on misbehavior in corporations or the government. It's led by David Ison, the dean of St. Paul's Cathedral, and Michael Woodford, the whistleblowing former CEO of Olympus, the Japanese corporation famous for its cameras. The commission's objective is to determine how public attitudes, laws, and rules about whistleblowing should be changed to encourage speaking up when people see wrongdoing.

At the same time, the U.K. Financial Conduct Authority (FCA), a quasi-governmental agency that was formed as one of the successors of the Financial Services Authority (FSA) and serves as a sort of counterpart to the U.S. SEC, is considering the adoption of U.S.-style bounty payments to whistleblowers, considering "the FSA receive[d] up to 4,000 whistleblowing reports every year, with 12% pursued as 'actionable intelligence.'" Martin Wheatley, chief executive designate of the FCA, told a Parliamentary commission that the FCA is looking into providing cash incentives, adding, "We have spoken to the U.S. authorities and are looking very carefully at it, but it is too early to make a judgment yet." He continued, "The key difference to us is the incentive structure. Under our system it is a moral incentive to do the right thing, whereas the U.S. system operates a financial incentive, and there are some pros and cons to both."

The *IMA® Statement of Ethical Professional Practice* provides guidance as to how an individual should proceed in notifying the proper person of wrongdoing. The IMA (Institute of Management Accountants) Ethics Helpline provides assistance—for members and nonmembers—in interpreting the *IMA Statement*. In serious cases, consider consulting an independent attorney before reporting incidents outside the organization.

New Whistleblower Rules Broaden Opportunities

When the Sarbanes-Oxley Act (SOX) was passed in 2002, it was expected that Section 806 of the Act, "Protection for Employees of Publicly Traded Companies Who Provide Evidence of Fraud," would motivate employees to blow the whistle on employers who committed fraudulent activities. The thinking involved prohibiting discriminatory acts against an employee who provided information about fraudulent activities in connection with financial disclosures of a public company, thus making it safer for employees to come forward and report wrongdoing. Remedies under the law include reinstatement and back pay, but employers face no penalties.

Section 806 has been largely unsuccessful in protecting reporting employees from retaliatory acts. Because employees must meet a very high burden of proof in order to win their case, employers have successfully challenged in court virtually all claims filed. The U.S. Department of Labor administers this portion of SOX, not the U.S. Securities & Exchange Commission (SEC). To remedy the shortcomings of SOX, the Dodd-Frank Wall Street Reform and Consumer Protection Act (DFA) passed in July 2010 enables cash motivations for whistleblowers who report violations of the securities laws. It also broadens the range of possible whistleblowers to include more than just employees.

After considering many public comments, the SEC just issued final rules effective August 2011 that enable it to pay substantial cash bounties to individuals who provide information about securities frauds. Awards to whistleblowers can range from 10% to 30% of the amount of monetary sanctions arising from SEC enforcement actions that result in more than $1 million in penalties, interest, and disgorgement of ill-gotten gains. Information provided to the SEC must be a voluntary act, "original," and derived from the whistleblower's independent knowledge or analysis and not known to the SEC from any other source.

"For an agency with limited resources like the SEC, it is critical to be able to leverage the resources of people who may have firsthand information about violations of the securities laws," SEC Chair Mary L. Schapiro said. "While the SEC has a history of receiving a high volume of tips and complaints, the quality of the tips we have received has been better since Dodd-Frank became law, and we expect this trend to continue."

One of the most troubling aspects of the whistleblower cash initiative in the Dodd-Frank Act was its perceived possible negative impact on public companies' internal compliance programs. Most large companies have instituted internal confidential reporting processes, or "hotlines," that comply with the mitigation provisions of the U.S. Sentencing Guidelines. People could choose to report wrongdoing to the SEC and obtain substantial cash rather than report internally and face possible reprisal. The final SEC rules don't include any explicit requirements that whistleblowers utilize internal reporting and compliance programs in order to be eligible for an award, but the rules do contain incentives to motivate whistleblowers to report to such systems when appropriate.

Incentives include providing for an increase in the amount awarded under the program when a whistleblower voluntarily participates in an organization's internal compliance system and a decrease in such amount for any interference with the entity's system. Additionally, all of the information provided by an entity's investigation of an issue will be attributed to a whistleblower and thus possibly increase the amount of the resulting award if the entity fully reports information to the SEC that leads to a successful action. The adopting release notes that "internal compliance programs are not substitutes for rigorous law enforcement."

Of course, employees won't always have confidence that their employer will promptly self-report to the SEC any possibly incriminating information received via an internal hotline. Important to the success of internal ethics and compliance programs is sufficient oversight by a committee of independent directors and participation by the full board when necessary. A number of companies have assigned this responsibility to the audit committee.

Factors to be considered in determining the percentage of the total SEC sanctions that would be awarded to a whistleblower are (1) significance of the information provided by the whistleblower, (2) assistance provided by the whistleblower, (3) law enforcement interest in making a whistleblower award, and (4) participation by the whistleblower in internal compliance systems. Criteria that may decrease a whistleblower's award percentage are (1) culpability of the whistleblower, (2) unreasonable reporting delay by the whistleblower, and (3) interference with internal compliance and reporting systems by the whistleblower.

For a whistleblower to be eligible for an award, the information provided must be sufficiently credible, specific, and timely to result in either an activation or reactivation of an SEC investigative process or "significantly contribute" to the success of an investigation already under way. Individuals already having a responsibility to report wrongdoing to the SEC are precluded from receiving monetary awards. Special provisions apply to reporting of information by either internal or external auditors.

Employees engaged in internal auditing or compliance processes and auditors engaged in an independent audit of the financial statements of a public company can be compensated as whistleblowers when:

- The whistleblower believes disclosure may prevent substantial injury to the financial interest or property of the entity or investors,

- The whistleblower believes that the entity is engaging in conduct that will impede an investigation, or

- At least 120 days have elapsed since the whistleblower reported the information to his or her supervisor or the entity's audit committee, chief legal officer, chief compliance officer—or at least 120 days have elapsed since the whistleblower received the information, if the whistleblower received it under circumstances indicating that these people are already aware of the situation.

The SEC believes that these stated conditions are a high bar that won't destroy the necessary open cooperation that every auditor requires in order to perform his or her job. The SEC's adopting release notes, "We believe it is in the public interest to accept whistleblower submissions

and to reward whistleblowers—whether they are officers, directors, auditors, or similar responsible personnel—who give us information that allows us to take enforcement action to prevent substantial injury to the entity or to investors." For some time, independent auditors have had the duty to report illegal conduct encountered during an audit.

External auditors engaged in an independent audit may also receive an award for blowing the whistle on their firm, even if doing so would breach a duty of confidentiality to a client. Specifically, a footnote to the adopting release states that the SEC wasn't excluding any information that "is received in breach of state-law confidentiality requirements, such as those imposed on auditors, because to do so could inhibit important federal-law enforcement interests." Additional requirements deal with attorney-client privilege.

A whistleblower who provides information to the SEC is protected from employment retaliation if the person possesses a "reasonable belief" that the information he or she is providing relates to a "possible" securities law violation that has occurred, is ongoing, or is about to occur. It's unlawful for a company to interfere with a whistleblower's efforts to communicate with the SEC by, for example, threatening to enforce a confidentiality agreement.

The whistleblower protection aspects are administered by the Occupational Safety & Health Administration (OSHA). A complaint of retaliation filed with OSHA must allege that the complainant engaged in protected activity, the respondent knew about that activity, the respondent subjected the complainant to an adverse action, and the protected activity motivated or contributed to the adverse action. Adverse action is generally defined as any action that would dissuade a reasonable employee from engaging in protected activity.

The SEC has established an Office of the Whistleblower and funded the Investor Protection Fund with $451.9 million as of the end of the government's 2010 fiscal year. A Tips, Complaints, and Referrals (TCR) report can be accepted by the SEC. TCR information is made available throughout the agency using a new $21 million TCR Database.

Tips and other inside information are the most important mechanism for detecting fraud. With all of the tools available, the SEC should be able to continue to bring significant cases of fraud to successful resolution. Ideally, their availability will act as a deterrent of additional fraud in the future.

Whistleblowers Need Encouragement, not Roadblocks

It's well understood that a whistleblower is the most important source of evidence in detecting fraud and other misdeeds and convicting the criminal or enforcing a civil statute. The whistleblower program at the U.S. Securities & Exchange Commission (SEC) has allowed many individuals to report securities laws violations. But companies and their counsel are reportedly impeding would-be whistleblowers in violation of the law. In addition, the Internal Revenue Service (IRS) and U.S. Commodity Futures Trading Commission (CFTC) whistleblower initiatives appear to require streamlining to improve their effectiveness.

The Dodd-Frank Act enables the SEC to pay cash to whistleblowers who report significant wrongdoing (more than $1 million in sanctions). In November 2012, then SEC Chairman Mary L. Schapiro reported, "In just its first year, the whistleblower program already has proven to be a valuable tool in helping us ferret out financial fraud. When insiders provide us with high-quality road maps of fraudulent wrongdoing, it reduces the length of time we spend investigating and saves the agency substantial resources."

The second cash award under the SEC's whistleblower program was announced June 12, 2013. The SEC will award three whistleblowers 15% of the total amount recovered by the government in return for tips and information they provided to help the SEC and the Justice Department stop a sham hedge fund. The total reward is expected to amount to approximately $125,000. Whistleblowers are paid from the SEC's Investor Protection Fund, which held more than $453 million at the end of the 2012 fiscal year.

Additional and larger awards are expected in the future. The SEC Office of the Whistleblower had posted 76 orders in 2013 (through August), each with monetary sanctions exceeding $1 million. These include well-known defendants such as U.S. technology company IBM, Dutch bank ABN AMRO, Swiss bank UBS Securities, and French oil company Total S.A. According to whistleblower attorney Jordan Thomas, "There has been a green line that financial services professionals have historically feared to cross, but they are now more willing to break their silence because of the SEC Whistleblower Program." He added, "In the coming years, I predict many of the SEC's most significant cases will be the result of whistleblowers who report their tips to the agency."

Obstacles

A court decision in Houston, Texas, involving General Electric (GE) may confound the protective rights of whistleblowers to be shielded from retaliatory acts of their employer. The plaintiff was a former executive at GE who alleged he was fired because he was a whistleblower. GE, however, claimed that the executive never reported it to the SEC, blurring the SEC's definition of a "whistleblower." The court stated that "without any allegation that he reported a securities-law violation to the SEC, [the plaintiff] is not a 'whistleblower' under Dodd-Frank." GE stated its "consistent position has been that employees should report internally first, with lawsuits and bounties reserved for instances where a company fails to respond appropriately, obliging employees to report to the SEC." The plaintiff's attorney is contemplating an appeal to the U.S. Supreme Court.

The case hinges on the issue of whether the Dodd-Frank Act protects whistleblowers in general or just those who report misdeeds to the SEC. Several courts held earlier that all whistleblowers were covered under Dodd-Frank and thus were protected from reprisal. It appears that whistleblowers need legal representation to help determine the appropriate strategy, as recommended by the *IMA® Statement of Ethical Professional Practice.*

Another potential obstacle to the effectiveness of the SEC's whistleblowing initiative was pointed out in a May 8, 2013, letter to the SEC from whistleblower attorneys David J. Marshall and Debra S. Katz. They assert that "companies routinely include in separation agreements [restrictions] that undercut Congress' purpose in creating the SEC's whistleblower-reward program:

1. The requirement that the whistleblower renounce the right to receive any award the SEC might make as the result of a successful enforcement action; and

2. Requirements that an employee disclose to the company all past or future communications with any third party, including government agencies, and/or that the employee agree to cooperate with the company in any ensuing investigation by the SEC."

According to Marshall and Katz, companies continue to devise ways to restrict whistleblowers despite SEC rules stating that "no person may take any action to impede an individual from communicating directly with the Commission staff about a possible securities law violation." They continued, "The inclusion of such terms in severance agreements and settlement agreements resolving employment claims has a chilling effect on individuals who would provide information to the SEC about potential securities violations." The SEC's discussion of its Final Rule under Dodd-Frank Section 21F states that Section 29(a) of the Exchange Act (of which the Dodd-Frank Act is a part) specifically states, "Employers may not require employees to waive or limit their anti-retaliation rights under Section 21F."

In their letter to the SEC, Marshall and Katz noted that employees may not have legal counsel or much time to decide whether to sign a severance agreement favorable to their employer. In their view, such pressure undermines the protections from retaliatory acts that Congress and the SEC intended to afford whistleblowers. They recommend the SEC issue clarifying regulations "to stem the growth of an apparent effort to discourage whistleblowers from providing information to the Commission," which is the clear objective of the SEC's whistleblower reward program.

More Encouragement Needed

The whistleblower program at the IRS revealed significant activity in its 2012 fiscal year annual report. There were 332 submissions, involving 671 taxpayers, that appeared to meet the statutory threshold of $2 million of tax, penalties, and interest in dispute. Awards of more than $125 million were paid during the year to 128 whistleblowers. In fiscal year 2013, the only publicly announced award under the revised 2006 statute was a payment of $104 million made to a former banker at Swiss UBS AG—the largest payment ever. The informant provided information that resulted in UBS turning over the names of thousands of Americans suspected of being tax cheats.

The IRS annual report raised concerns that it says need to be addressed to improve the whistleblower program:

1. Protection of whistleblowers against retaliation. There are no provisions similar to those in the Dodd-Frank Act.

2. Means of providing adequate protection of confidential information of taxpayers whose taxes are at issue.

3. Clarification of the definition of "amount in dispute" and how to determine the amount of "gross income." Also, an observer may wonder why the threshold of IRS interest is $2 million rather than the $1 million in the Dodd-Frank Act.

In addition, on August 29, 2013, U.S. Attorney General Eric Holder announced a new program to encourage Swiss banks to cooperate with ongoing investigations of the use of foreign bank accounts to commit tax evasion. The Swiss government announced it would encourage Swiss banks to cooperate. "This program will significantly enhance the Justice Department's ongoing efforts to aggressively pursue those who attempt to evade the law by hiding their assets outside of the United States," Holder said.

The CFTC also has a whistleblower program initiated by Dodd-Frank, but no awards have been paid yet. During fiscal year 2012, the whistleblower office received 58 complaints and an additional 52 tips that weren't whistleblowers. The whistleblower office has created an educational program to raise awareness of its whistleblower program. Like the SEC, the CFTC has a Customer Protection Fund, which held approximately $100 million at the end of fiscal 2012.

Whistleblowing's importance to all professional accountants is further emphasized in a proposed revision to the international *Code of Ethics for Professional Accountants* published by the International Ethics Standards Board for Accountants (IESBA). An exposure draft titled "Responding to a Suspected Illegal Act" was released in August 2012 and has drawn 73 comment letters, including one from IMA. The objective of the new pronouncement is to "describe the circumstances in which a professional accountant is required or expected to override confidentiality and disclose the act to an appropriate authority."

As companies try to restrict whistleblowers while government agencies and organizations try to encourage and protect them, it appears increasingly important that whistleblowers follow the guidance contained in the *IMA Statement of Ethical Professional Practice.* It recommends that when dealing with the resolution of ethical conflict, you "consult with your own attorney as to legal obligations and rights concerning the ethical conflict."

Retaliation for Whistleblowing Is on the Rise

Many favorable outcomes have resulted from the courageous actions of whistleblowers. Examples include the disclosures revealing the efforts of tobacco companies to get smokers hooked on nicotine, UBS's massive efforts to help U.S. taxpayers evade federal income taxes, and drug giant Pfizer's illegal marketing efforts that resulted in $2.3 billion of criminal and civil penalties. Unfortunately, those blowing the whistle on such events are likely to face the painful cost of retaliation.

The provisions of the Dodd-Frank Act that were enacted to encourage whistleblowers and protect them from retaliation are still being adjudicated in the court system. One recent case is *Kramer v. Trans-Lux Corp.*, Case No. 3:11-cv- 01424-SRU (D. Conn. September 25, 2012). The result was encouraging for whistleblowers. The U.S. District Court for Connecticut held that a whistleblower may pursue claims under the Sarbanes Oxley Act (SOX) as well as Dodd-Frank. The court also ruled that a whistleblower doesn't have to report a tip to the SEC in the manner prescribed by the SEC in order to qualify as a whistleblower under Dodd-Frank. Instead, the individual only must allege that he or she had a reasonable belief that the information relates to a possible violation of securities laws.

Though the courts continue to address the Dodd-Frank provisions, a report issued September 4, 2012, by the Ethics Resource Center (ERC) highlights the need for greater protection for whistleblowers. Titled *Retaliation: When Whistleblowers Become Victims,* the report details the practices of reporting illegal and unethical conduct in U.S. companies.

Retaliation analyzes data obtained in the 2011 National Business Ethics Survey (NBES), conducted before the protections of Dodd-Frank became effective. The NBES survey interviewed U.S. employees at all levels working at least 20 hours per week in the for-profit sector. Data was weighted for gender, age, and education.

According to ERC's *Retaliation* report, retaliation against workplace whistleblowers is now extending to previously safe groups such as senior managers and is involving more acts of physical violence. "Addressing workplace retaliation should be a high priority for business leaders," ERC President Patricia J. Harned said. "When an employee experiences retaliation for reporting misconduct, companies have two new problems. A second form of misconduct has been observed, and the reporter is now a victim. Additionally, retaliation can create an environment that is cancerous to the organization."

The rate of retaliation against whistleblowers is increasing far more quickly than the rate of people reporting misdoing. Since 2007, the rate of reporting misconduct, or whistleblowing, has increased from 58% of those who observe improper behavior to 65%. Of the reporting group, the rate of employees experiencing retaliation increased from 12% in 2007 to 22% in 2011. Among the unfavorable side effects of retaliation is the dampening of motivation for future whistleblowers and the increased risk that unreported wrongdoing will continue and expand because management has no opportunity to take corrective action.

Perhaps the most surprising findings set forth in *Retaliation* involve the striking increases in specific types of retaliatory acts—particularly those related to managerial employees. In the past two years alone, traceable retaliation (those that leave proof of having happened, such as physical harm, online harassment, harassment at home, job shift, demotion, or cuts to hours or pay) increased from 4% of those who experienced retaliation to 31%, managerial demotions increased from 18% to 32%, and relocations or reassignments increased from 27% to 44%.

This is the first time in the history of the ERC's studies of ethics that supervisory and managerial employees are now more likely to experience retaliation after whistleblowing. In addition, retaliation among union employees (another group with higher job security) increased dramatically in the past two years. Retaliation rates for union members were 25 percentage points higher (42%) than the rate for nonunion employees (17%).

Employees who feel comfortable enough to first report misconduct to their supervisor experience far less retaliation (17%) than those who first report to higher management (27%) or to their organization's hotline (40%). Possible explanations for this disparity are that (1) more significant violations would be reported to higher executives directly so that they could take immediate corrective action or (2) the reporter's supervisor may have some involvement with the situation. The severity of the wrongdoing also may be a factor here. Logically, more significant violations are more likely to result in retaliation. If the action being reported is serious enough that the reporting would be escalated above a supervisor or done through a hotline, it's also more likely that there would be retaliation for reporting that action. But in organizations with an open culture, speaking up to benefit the firm in the long run is more likely to be accepted.

The ERC report also shows a direct link between increased retaliation and job pressures or stress. Fifty-two percent of people who report wrongdoing and feel pressure to compromise standards also end up experiencing retaliation. But only 12% of those who didn't feel such pressures experience retaliation. This suggests that an open and ethically strong culture encourages whistleblowing, while an unethical culture is more likely to result in employees "going along to get along." The ERC study measures critical aspects of ethical culture, including management's trustworthiness, whether managers at all levels talk about ethics and model appropriate behavior, and the extent to which employees value and support ethical conduct, accountability, and transparency. Openness and the willingness to report misbehavior for the good of the organization is a positive outcome.

The best news in *Retaliation* is that ethics and compliance programs, strong ethical cultures, high standards of accountability that are applied consistently, and positive management behaviors are all linked to a reduced likelihood of retaliation. Though the rate of retaliation increased in stronger ethical cultures, that rate (15%) was still lower than the retaliation rate in ethically weak cultures, which increased to 27% from 24%. In addition, retaliation is lower in organizations with comprehensive ethics and compliance programs (2% of reporters) than it is in companies that lack all of the standard program elements (36%).

Using other measurements, retaliation is far less likely when employees agree that management is accountable. Managers also have the power to curb retaliation. When they are perceived as trustworthy and committed to ethics, retaliation is far less likely. Some of the measures of accountability include:

- Trust supervisor to keep promises and commitments,
- Trust top management to keep promises and commitments, and
- Trust coworkers to keep promises and commitments.

Retaliation includes additional recommendations from the ERC for organizations that want to reduce the likelihood of the damaging effects of retaliation for whistleblowers. They include:

- Assess the views of the organization regarding whistleblowing and the protection of those who come forward with concerns about actions they have observed.

- Target managers with antiretaliation training so they can recognize reporting, address the issues if possible, and interact with reporters in ways that aren't perceived as retaliatory.

- Communicate the reporting process broadly among all employees so they can feel reassured that progress is being made and are aware of the protections for those that do the reporting.

- Move investigations along and provide information as to the status of the issue so that reporters will feel they are being heard and won't need to bring up the same issues multiple times.

- Take steps to ensure that retaliation doesn't happen—show that fairness and consistency are the norms in the organization.

- Implement systems and procedures that ensure confidentiality.

- When a claim of retaliation is substantiated, take action in a way that is both decisive and, if possible, visible to employees.

- Track progress and periodically check up on reporters.

In view of the motivations for whistleblowing contained in Dodd-Frank—and the Act's greater protection against retaliation—the subject of whistleblowing and its influence in helping to establish and maintain a strong ethical culture within an organization deserves immediate attention and is likely to remain important for many years to come.

Responsibility Reporting Is Getting More Attention

Following the lead of European-based companies, companies in the United States and around the world increasingly report nonfinancial information addressing their impact on the environment and key stakeholders such as customers, suppliers, employees, the community, and the general public. The titles of these reports often include phrases such as "corporate responsibility" (CR), "sustainability," "environmental, social, and governance" (ESG), or "triple bottom line" (which includes economic, social, and environmental issues).

According to the *KPMG International Survey of Corporate Responsibility Reporting 2011,* corporate responsibility reporting has become a de facto standard for business, and it enhances the financial value of companies that do it. The KPMG survey analyzed the reports of more than 3,400 companies from 34 countries, including the 250 largest companies in the world (G250). Ninety-five percent of the G250 now report on their corporate responsibility activities, including almost 60% of China's largest companies that already report using corporate responsibility metrics. Of the G250 companies that don't report on corporate responsibility, two-thirds are based in the United States.

KPMG says, "With almost half of the largest companies already demonstrating financial gains from their CR initiatives, and with the increasing importance of innovation and learning as key drivers for reporting, it is clear that CR has moved from being a moral imperative to a critical business issue." Topping the list of business drivers motivating companies to report on their CR activities is reputational or brand considerations (cited by 67% of the G250), with ethical considerations also high on the list (58%).

Large, publicly held corporations have taken the lead in corporate responsibility reporting—with 70% doing so—but KPMG notes that other companies can benefit as well. The report states, "While family-owned and private equity-owned companies may face a different level of scrutiny than publicly traded companies, this does not exempt them from accounting for their positive and negative impacts on society, particularly in the modern information age."

The KPMG survey notes that 80% of G250 companies utilize the general guidelines for sustainability reporting published by the Global Reporting Initiative (GRI). The GRI guidelines suggest the areas of environmental, social, and governance topics that should be disclosed, but there's considerable variation in how much information companies report and how they report it. Efforts are under way to improve reporting. The GRI

is currently considering an updated fourth generation (G4) guidance document expected to be released sometime in 2013, and a group of business professionals has formed the U.S.-based Social Accountability Standards Board (SASB) with the aim "to develop reporting standards and benchmarks for environmental, social, and governance issues."

Thirty-five percent of G250 companies currently don't include information on corporate governance or control mechanisms in their CR reports. This has led one-third of the G250 companies to restate previously reported information. The practice of providing independent assurance is also quite divergent, with only 45% of all G250 companies—and only 13% of U.S. companies—engaging an external reviewer. Of those that undertake assurance, more than 70% engage major accounting organizations.

The BSR/GlobeScan *State of Responsible Business Poll 2012* reports that "companies can build trust by being increasingly transparent about business practices and by measuring and demonstrating positive social and environmental impacts." BSR, a U.S.-based nongovernmental organization (NGO) whose mission is to build a just and sustainable world, said respondents to the poll remained pessimistic about the amount of public trust in business. A total of 556 BSR members completed the survey: 51% from North America and 25% from Europe.

Respondents believe that the two areas in which business has made the most significant progress over the last 20 years are health and safety issues and sustainability reporting. Areas that have seen the least progress are sustainable consumption, particularly the use of water, and public policy. Those topics also are viewed as the greatest challenges for the future. Both the BSR and KPMG surveys suggest that the challenge of integrating sustainability into the core of business is a significant factor in making progress on sustainability issues.

Another indication of the popular interest surrounding sustainability in the business world is *Newsweek*'s annual calculation of companies' "green" performance. The fourth annual *Newsweek Green Rankings*® report utilizes the services of environmental research providers Trucost and Sustainanalytics to assess the performance of publicly traded U.S. and global corporations. Both the U.S. and global lists consist of a ranking by the "green score" of the largest 500 companies by revenue, market capitalization, and number of employees.

The green score is weighted 45% for environmental impact, 45% for environmental management, and 10% for environmental disclosure. The environmental impact is a comprehensive, quantitative, and standardized measure of approximately 700 metrics, including emissions of nine greenhouse gases, water use, solid-waste disposal, and emissions that contribute to acid rain and fog. Trucost uses company-reported and calculated direct and supply-chain quantitative data to determine an environmental damage cost based on a standardized cost per unit of input or output. This amount is normalized for company size.

The environmental management score is an assessment of how a company manages its environmental performance through policies, programs, targets, certifications, and the like. The composition of indicators and weightings used to evaluate a company varies by industry. All profiles are peer reviewed by Sustainanalytics internally and sent back to companies for verification. Half of the disclosure score is determined by each research provider. Trucost reflects the proportion of environmental impacts a company is disclosing out of those that are relevant. Sustainanalytics assesses the breadth and quality of environmental reporting as determined by the level of reported involvement in key transparency initiatives.

Analyzing the rankings of U.S. companies revealed some interesting industry patterns. The greenest industries in the U.S. were information technology and services, where 11 of 29 companies in the 500 (37.9%) were ranked in the top 10%; technology equipment, where 13 of 37 (35.1%) were ranked in the top 10%; and telecommunications, where two of nine (22.2%) were ranked in the top 10%. Industries that had the largest proportion of companies ranked in the bottom 10% were utilities, with 11 of 27 (40.7%), and materials, with 10 of 34 (29.4%). The other industries had companies dispersed throughout the rankings.

Despite all this attention, though, recent events show that there is room for improvement in corporate responsibility reporting. One example is the chain of events involving Barclays PLC, Britain's second-largest bank and a longtime advocate of good corporate citizenship. Its *2011 Annual Report* notes that "Citizenship is one of Barclays four execution priorities and is integral to its business." The report also quotes former CEO Bob Diamond, who said, "Banks need to become better citizens. This is not about philanthropy—it's about delivering real commercial benefits in a way that also creates value for society."

But shortly after publishing its near-100-page *Citizenship Report 2011* in April 2012, Barclays was fined £290 million ($451.4 million), the largest penalty ever assessed by U.S. and U.K. financial regulators. Barclays admitted submitting false information about its interbank borrowing rates that masked the bank's true financial health and increased trading profits, and Diamond was forced to resign.

In a story titled "Has Barclays brought corporate responsibility reporting into disrepute?" the U.K.-based *Guardian Sustainable Business Blog* described "the vast gap between the company's behavior and its so-called corporate sustainability aims." The story noted that this event "not only puts the value of corporate sustainability reporting in general into question, but also begs the question of whether independent social auditing is ever going to do more than just gloss over the surface of a company's affairs." Ernst & Young, who provided the assurance on Barclays's responsibility reporting, was also called to task by the blog: "Ernst & Young (E&Y) needs to recognize that by putting their official stamp on corporate responsibility reports, they give the very strong impression to stakeholders that all is well."

A three-page assurance report by E&Y says that the firm planned and performed its engagement in accordance with International Standard on Assurance Engagements (ISAE) 3000 and also standard AA1000AS issued by the Institute of Social and Ethical Accountability.

According to paragraph 49j of ISAE 3000, the practitioner's conclusion "should be expressed in the negative form." In other words, the practitioner should attest that nothing came to its attention that caused it to believe that the company's assertion(s), based on stated criteria, is stated unfairly. Yet there's no such language in the E&Y report on Barclays. Rather, E&Y's stated conclusions are positive and grouped into four categories: Inclusivity, Materiality, Responsiveness, and Completeness and Accuracy. There's no language to indicate that E&Y expresses any exception to any of the contents of the *Citizenship Report*.

Adding to the ethical challenges at Barclays is the announcement on November 1, 2012, that it's facing a double-barreled assault from U.S. authorities. The bank disclosed that it was facing a U.S. anticorruption investigation and that the U.S. Federal Energy Regulatory Commission is seeking a record $470 million in penalties for the bank's alleged manipulation of U.S. electricity markets.

While responsibility reporting is becoming more widespread among companies and drawing increased interest from the media, the events at Barclays suggest that more development and refinement are needed before responsibility reporting—and appropriate independent assurance—can provide the ethically related information that stakeholders require. Assurance providers should adhere to professional standards to avoid unwarranted conclusions by readers.

Sustainability as a Strategy

The debate about whether sustainable socially and environmentally responsible corporations report more favorable financial results for shareowners has carried on for many years.

Studies have already shown that highly motivated, more productive employees lead to lower turnover and training costs as well as an improved bottom line. In addition, investments in local charitable organizations and other efforts to burnish reputation also appear to result in positive returns. But the most difficult connection to demonstrate is that customers are willing to pay more for a product made by a company that at least tries to achieve broad social good. Now a recent survey by global consumer research firm Nielsen Holdings N.V. indicates a strong link between consumer actions and their wishes for positive social impact.

The survey report, "Doing Well by Doing Good," is based on an online poll of 30,000 respondents in 60 countries. The purpose of the survey is to ascertain:

- "How passionate consumers are about sustainable practices when it comes to purchase considerations.

- "Which consumer segments are most supportive of ecological or other socially responsible efforts.

- "The social issues/causes that are attracting the most concern."

The methodology for the study includes consideration of age and gender for each country based on its internet users, and it's weighted to be representative of internet consumers. It's based on claimed behavior rather than objective measurement.

Willing to Spend More

The findings show that 55% of global respondents "say they are willing to pay extra for products and services from companies that are committed to positive social and environmental impact." This is an increase from 50% in 2012 and 45% in 2011. The Asia-Pacific (64%), Latin America (63%), and Middle East/Africa (63%) regions express a stronger willingness than the global average. These percentages have increased nine, 13, and 10 percentage points, respectively, since 2011. While the purchasing sentiment in North America (42%) and Europe (40%) is lower than the

global average, these regions have increased seven and eight percentage points, respectively, since 2011.

The survey found similar results to a question about whether consumers had made a recent purchase from a socially responsible company. "More than half of global respondents (52%) say they have purchased at least one product or service in the past six months from a socially responsible company, with respondents in Latin America (65%), Asia-Pacific (59%) and Middle East/Africa (59%) exceeding the global average. Four in 10 respondents in North America and Europe say they have made a sustainable purchase in the past six months." Nielsen Holdings supported these conclusions by reviewing comparative retail sales data relating to 34 brands in nine countries.

Importance of Responsible Companies

Other corporate initiatives to protect the environment, be sustainable, and act in socially responsible ways also are important to consumers. Globally, two-thirds of respondents prefer to work for a socially responsible company, 53% check information on product packaging to ensure sustainable impact, and 49% volunteer with and/or donate to organizations engaged in social and environmental programs.

Amy Fenton, Nielsen's global leader of public development and sustainability, provides a conclusion as to the importance of companies acting responsibly: "At the moment of truth—in store, online and elsewhere—consumers are making a choice and a choice that is heavily influenced by brands with a social purpose." She adds, "This behavior is on the rise, and we are seeing this manifest into positive impact in our communities as well as share growth for brands."

Generational Responses

Nielsen's business collaborator Natural Marketing Institute (NMI) performed a separate nine-country online study looking at the ages at which customers are more likely to respond favorably to sustainability efforts. The goal was "to separate the passive eco-friendly consumer from the passionate [one]" and to better "understand how global attitudes and behaviors are changing with regard to sustainability engagement."

Millennials (ages 21-34) are by far the most responsive to sustainable companies with goals to serve all stakeholders—social and environmental as well as financial. Of the Millennial respondents, 51% pay extra for sustainable products, 51% check packaging to ensure positive environmental impact, and 49% prefer to work for a sustainable company. Generation X (ages 35-49) respondents are the next most responsive (25%, 25%, and 26%, respectively). Respondents in the Silent Generation (age 65 and older) are least responsive (3%, 2%, and 3%, respectively).

Fenton emphasizes the importance of brand promotion of sustainability: "Precision marketing and knowing your consumers intimately will yield the greatest results. It's no longer a question if consumers care about social impact. Consumers do care and show they do through their actions. The question is 'how is your brand effectively creating shared value by marrying the appropriate social cause and consumer segments?'"

Areas of Concern

Half or more of global consumers list six causes as areas of extreme concern. They are increasing access to clean water, improving access to sanitation, eradicating extreme poverty and hunger, combating noncommunicable diseases, ensuring environmental sustainability, and reducing child mortality.

For companies that want to incorporate efforts to address some of these areas into their practices, the study concludes that a five-part approach is required for success in utilizing sustainability as a brand strategy:

1. "VISION. Be clear, actionable and global.

2. ENDORSEMENT. Get adoption and action from senior leadership.

3. STRATEGY. Focus on outward messaging and consistent cause messaging.

4. ACCOUNTABILITY. Use key performance indicators, internally and externally.

5. MEASUREMENT. Quantify program outcomes and return on investment consistently across markets."

Integrated Reporting Lags in the U.S.

Efforts have been under way for years to make the reporting of corporate performance in both financial and nonfinancial terms more understandable and useful to all stakeholders. This is becoming even more difficult in today's business environment. Factors such as the growing complexity of doing business in a worldwide economy, the increased legal exposure of businesses in meeting regulatory requirements, and the move toward harmonizing accounting standards globally while still addressing the needs of local jurisdictions and regulatory agencies combine to create additional challenges in communicating performance results. And that's before you even factor in the growing popularity of corporate responsibility reporting and the expanded definition of a company's stakeholders.

In recent years, an initiative known as Integrated Reporting (IR), has focused on combining financial reporting with responsibility reporting concerning social issues, governance, and the environment. This movement is led by the International Integrated Reporting Council (IIRC), which issued the *International Integrated Reporting Framework* (IIRF) in 2013 to set guidelines for reporting. According to the IIRC, "An integrated report is a concise communication about how an organization's strategy, governance, performance and prospects, in the context of its external environment, lead to the creation of value over the short, medium and long term."

IR aspires to greater benefits for all stakeholders whose companies adopt the practice. The IIRC believes it "is a process founded on integrated thinking that results in a periodic integrated report by an organization about value creation over time and related communications regarding aspects of value creation." Because of its future orientation and emphasis on value creation, investors should be able to better understand company strategies and how effectively they work, resulting in lower costs of capital for the organization over the long term. Internally, a common focus on creation of long-term value with consideration of environmental and social issues should eliminate thinking in silos and result in a more effective and efficient execution of long-term strategies.

The IIRC published a summary of progress in 2012-2013 reported by the 100 companies in the Pilot Programme—companies that volunteered to implement the principles of the Framework. Its "Business and Investors Explore the Sustainability Perspective of Integrated Reporting" report found that businesses in the IIRC Pilot Programme are tackling key interconnected areas of IR: the use of capitals, the creation of value, and the definition of the organization's business model.

According to Mervyn E. King, chairman of the IIRC, "Integrated Reporting is playing a role in meeting the world's two great challenges—financial stability and sustainability. The participants in the IIRC Pilot Programme have made and continue to make an important contribution to sustainable capitalism."

IR in the U.S.

Historically, the emphasis of corporate reporting in the United States has been on meeting quarterly earnings expectations and satisfying shareholders. The movement to address stakeholders beyond investors is gaining strength, but it still lags behind other countries. Consistent with that trend, only seven of the companies in the IIRC's Pilot Programme have their corporate headquarters in the U.S. In an online search, I was only able to find integrated reporting information for two of those companies.

The first company is Jones Lang LaSalle Incorporated (JLLI), a global financial and professional services firm specializing in commercial real estate services and investment management. JLLI's 2013 Annual Report to the Securities & Exchange Commission (SEC) on Form 10-K contains a paragraph stating the company intended the report to satisfy the requirements of the IIRF, presumably by combining both financial and sustainability reporting. Nevertheless, JLLI published both a 2013 Sustainability Report and a 2013 Transparency Report. This limited coverage doesn't seem to be a ringing endorsement of actually integrating corporate responsibility reporting with financial reporting.

The second company is Clorox Corp., a multinational manufacturer and marketer of consumer and professional cleaning/household products. Of the U.S. companies in the IIRC's Pilot Programme, Clorox has made the most substantial effort at integrated reporting so far. But a look at the results shows that more progress is needed.

Clorox Corp.'s Integrated Report

An August 1, 2014, press release presented Clorox's fiscal year 2014 financial results. This document followed usual public company practices and wasn't prepared as an integrated report. A separate press release on October 13, 2014, announced the publication of Clorox's 2014 Integrated Annual Report. Yet the release contained no financial information or integrated disclosures. It highlights the four factors helping Clorox achieve its fiscal year 2014 business and corporate responsibility objectives—Engage Employees, Innovate Every Day, Expand Our Brands, and Fund Growth—which are contained in the context of the company's 2020 Strategy:

- "Engage our people as business owners"—Using consulting firm data for workforce attitudes and reported U.S. government safety experience, Clorox has empowered its employees to streamline operational processes and make decisions faster. Its safety record is world class.

- "Increase brand investment behind superior value and more targeted 3D innovation"—This year, the company saw sustainability improvements in 15% of its products, and promotional efforts emphasized value.

- "Grow in profitable new categories, channels and countries"—Expansion plans during the year targeted new products and new markets.

- "Fund growth by reducing waste in our work, products and supply chain"—This was the 11th consecutive year that Clorox had cost savings in excess of $100 million. The company reduced its greenhouse gases by 12% and its waste sent to landfills per product unit by 34%.

Clorox's 2014 Integrated Annual Report is presented in a digital format that utilizes the forward-looking principles of IR. It uses the context of Clorox's 2020 Strategy to measure the company's performance in the current year in terms of financial, environmental, social, and governance factors. The strategies are repeated under the general caption of the Integrated Business Model—Goal, Mission, Objective, and Commitment.

The Integrated Annual Report has a Scorecard section containing five subcategories and a company profile that gives a short summation of the report. Each subcategory has quantitative measures of 2014 achievements, several of which have review-level negative assurance by Clorox's independent public accounting firm, Ernst & Young.

The Performance (or financial) subcategory of the report contains four measures based on Generally Accepted Accounting Principles (GAAP) and three non-GAAP measures. A footnote page explains the non-GAAP measures: EBIT (earnings before interest and taxes), Economic Profit, and Free Cash Flow. The other subcategories are Products ("Making responsible products, responsibly"), Planet ("shrinking our environmental footprint while growing our business"), People ("Engaging our people as business owners and promoting diversity, opportunity and respectful treatment"), and Our Impact ("Safeguarding families with our Be healthy, Be smart and Be safe initiatives").

Clorox's Financial Reporting

The Clorox 2014 Annual Report to the SEC on Form 10-K appears straightforward and has the same regulatory format as other U.S. public companies, but it excludes a great deal of financial information that many companies would include. Clorox has an Appendix in its Proxy Statement containing the Management's Discussion and Analysis of Financial Condition and Results of Operations, audited financial statements, the independent auditor's opinion on the financial statements and internal control over financial reporting, and other selected financial information. These separate documents are required disclosures that most companies put in their 10-K, not in their Proxy Statement. There was no mention of Integrated Reporting in either Clorox's 2014 Proxy Statement or its Annual Report on Form 10-K. A reconciliation schedule explained the differences between GAAP income and economic income, but the heading didn't mention GAAP. Neither was there any mention of the other two non-GAAP financial measures reported in the Clorox Integrated Annual Report.

The end result is two separate reports describing Clorox's performance for the year. The major goal of IR is to align various frameworks for nonfinancial reporting and integrate them or connect them directly to financial measures to better inform investors and other market constituents about the long-term, sustainable value-creation capability of the organization. Having two unconnected, distinct reports doesn't seem to fulfill that goal.

IR and Ethical Behavior

In this column, I have long advocated that companies that behave ethically generally report better results, and the evidence continues to support that notion. One element of behaving ethically is the consideration of other key stakeholders beyond the company's shareowners. This includes the employees; the cities, towns, and other locales in which the company operates; and the environment. As seen in Clorox's 2014 Integrated Annual Report, an important aspect of IR is corporate responsibility and/or sustainability reporting. Thus, companies that embrace IR would appear to be moving in the right direction of ethical behavior by establishing a company culture that looks to long-term growth and sustainability and values the needs of all stakeholders over short-term gains.

Unfortunately, the examples from two of the U.S. companies in the IIRC's Pilot Programme appear to fall short of meaningful Integrated Reporting. The creation of two different reports—one that gets filed with the SEC and another that's published separately—raises the question of whether IR is possible within the regulatory environment. Are other solutions, such as reducing the excessive disclosures required by regulators, needed before IR can gain a stronger foothold in the U.S.?

Maximizing Returns or Unethical Tax Avoidance?

The furor over the extensive tax-avoidance measures used by technology companies such as Google and Apple has reached new heights in both the United Kingdom and the United States. Government members from both countries recently accused the two tech giants of scheming to avoid paying taxes. When this kind of news breaks, most companies respond by saying they must do everything possible to maximize net profits for shareowners, but the countries that miss out on the tax revenue based on profits they believe were generated within their borders argue that these companies are being unethical and possibly skirting the law. Critics maintain that high taxes on repatriating profits to the U.S. exacerbate the problem and encourage overseas investment to the detriment of employment at home.

During a Parliament committee hearing in the U.K., Margaret Hodge, chair of the Public Accounts Committee (PAC), accused Google of "devious, calculating, and unethical" behavior. Hodge alleged that the company marketed its product in the U.K. but used "smoke and mirrors to avoid paying tax" there. "You are a company that says you do no evil, and I think that you do do evil," Hodge told Matt Brittin, Google's vice president for sales and operations in northern Europe.

Google vigorously denied it avoided taxes by disguising the real nature of its business in the U.K. The company asserted that it did pay tax on profits from its services provided to affiliated entities but that the profits on the bulk of its business—sales to U.K. retail customers—were actually transacted in Ireland and that it didn't sell product from London. The head tax partner at Ernst & Young, however, told the hearing that an Irish resident company could be deemed to be trading in Britain if U.K.-based employees had habitually concluded deals on behalf of an Irish company. Hodge replied that "if sales activity is taking place in the U.K....you are misleading both Parliament and the tax authorities in suggesting that is not happening."

In the U.S., the Senate Permanent Subcommittee on Investigations held hearings at which Apple CEO Tim Cook defended the company's practice of paying no U.S. income tax on Apple operations outside the country. Cook strenuously asserted that the company paid its tax bill in full for all of its domestic operations. In the case of foreign operations, however, Apple utilizes avoidance provisions in the Irish tax law to the full extent, as do many other companies. As hard as it is to believe, Apple has been able to create corporations that pay no income tax to any taxing nation. This is possible because Ireland doesn't assess income tax on entities that are managed from outside the country, and the U.S. assesses taxes based on the country of subsidiary incorporation only.

These issues have become more prominent as the technological advances of recent years enable "remote control" management of a corporation. Directors meetings and other legally determined functions for Apple's Irish holding company subsidiary, Apple Operations International (AOI), were held in California. AOI has no employees and no physical presence in Ireland, being entirely managed and operated from the United States. Apple's U.S. service center in Austin, Texas, does the entity's accounting, and another Apple subsidiary in Nevada manages finances. The assets are held in a bank account in New York.

The importance of intellectual property to the profitability of tech companies has made them the focus of governments looking into the alleged shifting of profits to low-tax countries. According to Senator Carl Levin (D.-Mich.), chair of the Investigating subcommittee, those "profits depend on the ideas that bring [physical] elements together in such an elegant package. That intangible genius is intellectual property that is nurtured and developed here in the United States."

He continued, "[Intellectual property] is also highly mobile—unlike more tangible, physical assets, its value can be transferred around the globe, often with just a few keystrokes."

Apple's statement to the subcommittee explained the company's belief in no uncertain terms that it wasn't a tax evader: "Apple does not use tax gimmicks. Apple does not move its intellectual property into offshore tax havens and use it to sell products back into the U.S. in order to avoid U.S. tax; it does not use revolving loans from foreign subsidiaries to fund its domestic operations; it does not hold money on a Caribbean island; and it does not have a bank account in the Cayman Islands. Apple has substantial foreign cash because it sells the majority of its products outside the U.S."

The subcommittee's description of Apple's strategies was quite different: "Apple Inc., a U.S. corporation, has used a variety of offshore structures, arrangements, and transactions to shift billions of dollars in profits away from the United States and into Ireland, where Apple appears to have negotiated a special corporate tax arrangement of less than 2%. Despite reporting net income of $30 billion over the four-year period 2009 to 2012, AOI paid no corporate income taxes to any national government during that period. Similarly, Apple Sales International [ASI], a second Irish affiliate, is the repository for Apple's offshore intellectual property rights and the recipient of substantial income related to Apple worldwide sales, yet claims to be a tax resident nowhere and may be causing that income to go untaxed."

ASI purchases finished products from Chinese manufacturing corporations and then resells them to other Apple marketing affiliates around the world at a substantial markup. Ireland allows Apple to record virtually all of its profits from these transactions in that country based on a cost-sharing arrangement set up when the economic benefits of intellectual properties were transferred there years ago. It appears that only products destined for countries outside the U.S. market use this procedure.

The subcommittee's statement concluded that "Apple makes use of multiple U.S. tax loopholes, including the check-the-box rules, to shield offshore income otherwise taxable under Subpart F. Those loopholes have enabled Apple, over a four-year period from 2009 to 2012, to defer paying U.S. taxes on $44 billion of offshore income, or more than $10 billion of offshore income per year. As a result, Apple has continued to build up its offshore cash holdings which now exceed $102 billion."

Subpart F of the Internal Revenue Code was enacted some 50 years ago to forestall the increased use of tax-haven subsidiaries by U.S. corporations. Regulations designed to require "market-based" transfer prices between affiliates are now less effective because of the unique qualities of technology-based products and less frequent transfers of physical goods. According to the Internal Revenue Service's (IRS) testimony at the subcommittee hearing, "the check-the-box regulations provide that an eligible foreign entity with a single owner can be treated as 'disregarded' as a separate entity." The result is that many U.S. companies prefer to hold cash overseas rather than repatriate it back to the U.S. and incur income tax at what they perceive to be a very high rate. According to Joe Rosenberg, U.S. corporations hold more than $1 trillion in subsidiaries incorporated in countries with lower tax rates ("Let Apple and Microsoft Bail Out Uncle Sam," *The Wall Street Journal,* May 16, 2013).

Unfortunately, there's no international organization with the ability to harmonize tax laws on a global basis. Each sovereign nation's structures its tax laws to accomplish the objectives of raising revenue while protecting its own particular economic interests. As a consequence, countries compete against each other for tax revenue, and companies take advantage of it. One country's pain from not collecting taxes it believes result from economic activity within its borders is another country's success in using its own unique strategies to be an economic attraction. A study by the Organisation for Economic Cooperation and Development (OECD), commissioned by the G20 nations, finds that these tax avoidance strategies, "though technically legal, erode the tax base of many countries and threaten the stability of the international tax system," according to OECD Secretary-General
Angel Gurría.

The tech companies aren't alone in sheltering income from U.S. taxation. Presently, most corporations feel no obligation to help solve the fiscal problems of any country they do business in. They believe their only responsibility is to maximize return to their shareowners, and the compensation of most CEOs and senior executives is based primarily on short-term financial performance. A solution to this problem involves motivating the investment community to place more emphasis on a company's nonfinancial obligations to all of its stakeholders. Fortunately, the reporting of sustainability information by corporations is increasing.

Six Unethical Practices that Need to Stop

In the United States over the past few decades, the most well-to-do people—the "1%"—have garnered an increasingly disproportionately large share of the nation's assets, concentrating greater and greater wealth in the hands of fewer and fewer people. The 2013 Federal Reserve Board Survey of Consumer Finances shows that the richest 3% of U.S. households own 54.4% of the nation's wealth, which is more than double the total wealth of the poorest 90% of families. The top 10% hold nearly 85% of the nation's wealth, whereas the bottom 50% only own 0.8%.

A graphic in the *The Boston Globe*'s 2015 Divided Nation Series illustrates the trend favoring the ultra-wealthy. It shows that in 1978, the top 0.1% of the U.S. population held 7.1% of the wealth, but that swelled to 22% of the wealth in 2012 as economic gains flowed to investors and financial service providers. In 2012, the top 0.1% of the population represented about 160,000 families with net wealth above $20.6 million. The share of U.S. wealth of the top 10% declined from 81.9% to 79.2%, but the portion held by the lower 99% of that group fell from 74.8% to 55.2%. During this same period, the share of the least wealthy 90% dropped from approximately 28.1% to 22.8%, reflecting stagnation in wage growth.

Such a concentration of wealth has more potential adverse effects than envy and social unrest. According to the Institute for Policy Studies (IPS), recent research reveals that extreme wealth inequality may be having a negative effect on the health and longevity of Americans.

How did this happen?

A December 29, 2015, article in *The New York Times* titled "For the Wealthiest, A Private Tax System That Saves Them Billions" stated that "the wealthy have used their influence to steadily whittle away at the government's ability to tax them." The result has been much lower tax payments by the ultrarich. The newspaper reported that 20 years ago "the 400 highest-earning taxpayers in America paid nearly 27 percent of their income in federal taxes, according to IRS data. By 2012…that figure had fallen to less than 17 percent, which is just slightly more than [that paid by] the typical family making $100,000 annually, when payroll taxes are included for both groups."

What must we do?

To start reversing this dangerous trend, we must stop six key unethical practices.

1. **Eliminate the "carried interest" tax provisions.** "Carried interest" is a term used to describe the bonus-incentive performance fee paid to managers of hedge and private equity funds to reward them for superior performance. The U.S. Internal Revenue Code (IRC) specifically taxes this income at the long-term capital gains rate (a maximum of 15%) rather than the ordinary income rate (a maximum of 39.6%). In addition, fund managers usually receive a flat-rate management fee, normally 2% of assets under management, which is taxed as ordinary income.

2. **Effectively cap tax deductibility of excessive executive compensation.** The IRC prohibits corporations from deducting executive salaries exceeding $1 million. This has resulted in compensation for senior executives being based largely on short-term and noneconomic measures of "performance" that may be detrimental to the company. Use of unaudited, self-determined performance goals for bonuses instead of financial results reported to shareowners can ensure payment of bonuses to executives regardless of whether the outcome really is favorable for shareowners or whether the executive contributed to achieving the outcome.

3. **Raise the holding period for gains considered long-term.** Currently, a capital asset needs to be held for one year

before the gains on its sale can be preferentially taxed at the long-term capital gains rates of 0%, 15%, or 20% rather than at the short-term gains rates of 10%-39.6%. No informed individual considers a year to be a long-term for an investment, but the nearly two-thirds saving in taxes has strongly motivated corporate executives to be paid in stock rather than cash.

Companies may use cash to repurchase shares from the public to increase earnings per share outstanding rather than investing in a long-term strategy. Focusing on short-term results that support share prices or "quarterly capitalism" can lead to management of earnings to meet short-term expectations. Lifting the holding period for preferential tax treatment of gains by at least two or three years would direct management to focus more on the longer-term sustainability of the enterprise.

4. **Restrict transfers of wealth to tax havens.** Research by University of California-Berkeley economist Gabriel Zucman reveals that as much as $7.6 trillion—or 8% of the world's total financial wealth—is believed to be hidden from view worldwide and isn't being taxed. The annual effect on government revenues is significant. Zucman believes tax evasion by individuals costs governments $200 billion a year, and tax-saving strategies by U.S. multinational companies cost the U.S. government $130 billion annually.

In an interview with Jesse Drucker for a September 21, 2015, Bloomberg.com article, Zucman said that the need to stop the wave of tax avoidance and evasion goes beyond the revenue lost to the particular dodges. "If a significant fraction of rich people can evade taxes and if the rest of the population feels taxes are not fairly enforced, then the willingness to pay taxes will disappear," Zucman asserted.

5. **Reduce tax subsidies for home ownership.** Increasing home ownership has been a worthwhile objective for many years, yet wealthy individuals receive subsidies in the form of tax deductibility for second homes only they can afford. Further, a cap should be placed on the tax deductibility of mortgages now subsidizing the ownership of residences of extremely high value.

6. **Eliminate unlimited retirement contributions for the wealthy only.** "A Tale of Two Retirements," co-published on October 28, 2015, by IPS and the Center for Effective Government (CEG), reported that CEOs of *Fortune* 500 companies have been able to set aside before-tax funds of $3.2 billion in special tax-deferred compensation accounts that are exempt from the annual contribution limits imposed on ordinary individuals' 401(k)s. The CEOs don't have to pay any income tax until they withdraw from the accounts after retirement. In 2014 alone, these CEOs saved $78 million on their tax bills by putting $197 million more in these tax-deferred accounts than they could have if they were subject to the same rules as other workers. Almost half of total retirement assets for *Fortune* 500 CEOs are in the form of deferred compensation.

Stopping these practices will require strong Congressional leadership, but implementing them will help society avoid a growing, serious problem.

Ethical Behavior Differs Among Generations

In June, the Ethics Resource Center (ERC) published a new study that provides further analysis of its 2011 *National Business Ethics Survey* (NBES). The Washington, D.C.-based ERC is a private, nonprofit organization devoted to independent research and the advancement of high ethical standards and practices in public and private organizations. The initial analysis of the 2011 NBES showed unexpected and disturbing findings that may portend a future downward shift in business ethics. This new report, titled *Generational Differences in Workplace Ethics,* examines the differences in attitudes toward ethical issues among the four generational groups.

Demographics

The four generational groups examined in the survey are Traditionalists, Baby Boomers, Generation X workers (Gen Xers), and Millennials or Generation Y workers (Gen Yers). Traditionalists, born 1925-1945, are hardworking, respectful of authority, and value loyalty. Baby Boomers, born 1946-1964, are hardworking, idealistic, and committed to harmony. Gen Xers, born 1965-1980, are entrepreneurial, flexible and self-reliant, and comfortable with technology. Millennials, born 1981-2000, are tech-savvy, appreciative of diversity, and skilled in multitasking.

Some of the negative traits and workplace attributes widely assigned to each cohort include:

• Traditionalists—Conformers who resist change, are disciplined and pragmatic, work and family lives never coincide, dress formally.

• Boomers—Self-centered with sense of entitlement, workaholics, self-motivated, don't appreciate feedback.

• Gen Xers—Lazy, skeptical and cynical, question authority figures, desire for a work-life balance and flexible schedule, work dress is at low end of business casual.

• Millennials—Lack basic literacy fundamentals, very short attention spans, not loyal to organization, demand immediate feedback and recognition, integrate technology into the workplace, expect to have many employers and multiple careers, work dress is whatever feels comfortable.

Reporting and Its Consequences

According to *Generational Differences in Workplace Ethics,* these differences in attitudes and traits have resulted in a great deal of variability in many of the measures of workplace ethics. The study found that the youngest workers are significantly more likely than their older colleagues to feel pressure from others to break ethical rules because the pressure "eases as workers spend more time in the workforce and learn ways of coping with their work environment." As a possible solution, companies should concentrate more on issues of ethical culture during the orientation of new employees, which should mitigate their feeling of not knowing much about how to act within the culture of their new workplace.

Another finding in the generational study was that more younger workers have observed ethical misconduct in the workplace during the previous 12 months than their older colleagues. This is in spite of the fact that Millennials observed significantly fewer examples of using company time to conduct personal business than did those in older generations. The study explains this latter phenomenon by noting that younger workers tend to integrate their work and personal lives to a greater extent.

While earlier studies have shown that younger workers were less likely to report unethical behavior, the latest report shows a sharp increase in Millennials' reporting. "They are now on par with their older cohorts, except for Traditionalists," who observed and reported fewer instances than in previous years. Millennials observed 49% of workplace misconduct, the highest of all generations. The types of misconduct observed include:

• Personal business on company time—26%,

• Lying to employees—22%,

• Abusive behavior—21%,

• Company resource abuse—21%, and

• Discrimination—18%.

Of those Millennials who observed unethical behavior, 67% of them reported the misconduct, which included:

• Stealing or theft—74%,

• Falsifying expense reports—71%,

• Goods/services fail to meet specifications—69%,

• Falsifying time sheets or hours worked—68%, and

• Offering improper payments/bribes to public officials—67%.

All age groups tend to inform their supervisors, whom they know well and can trust, about misconduct they observed. Only a small percentage of workers went outside their organizations with their initial complaints. Millennials are the group most likely to report by using the hotline option. The study found that younger workers were significantly more likely than those in older generations to feel some form of retribution or retaliation. This is possibly due to the increase in their reporting of misdeeds.

Millennials: The Future of Professionalism

Perhaps the most surprising and disturbing result in the generational analysis is the relatively high percentages of Millennials who consider certain behaviors in the workplace to be ethical:

- Use social networking to find out about the company's competitors–37%,
- "Friend" a client or customer on a social network–36%,
- Upload personal photos on a company network–26%,
- Keep copies of confidential documents–22%,
- Work less to compensate for cuts in benefits or pay–18%,
- Buy personal items using a company credit card–15%,
- Blog or tweet negatively about a company–14%,
- Take a copy of work software home for personal use–13%.

The extensive use of social networking seems to pose challenges as significant numbers of Millennials post questionable information on their personal social networking sites:

- Feelings about their jobs–40%,
- Bad joke told by the boss–26%,
- Work on a project–26%,
- Picture of a coworker drinking–22%,
- Annoying habit of a coworker–20%,
- Information about the company's competitors–19%,
- Opinion about a coworker's politics–16%.

Most importantly, the report states that younger workers are significantly more willing to ignore the presence of misconduct if they think that behavior will help save jobs. "Willingness to 'let the ends justify the means' seems to have a strong inverse correlation with age," according to the report.

Building a Strong Ethics and Compliance Program

The most encouraging news in the new ERC study is that a robust ethical culture means less pressure to compromise standards, fewer observations of misconduct, higher rates of reporting, and decreased levels of retaliation against those who report. A strong ethics and compliance program has a significant role in developing and maintaining an organization's culture. In terms of the generations, Millennials are particularly driven by a strong program to be more proactive in their ethical conduct. Yet a weak ethics and compliance program has an adverse effect on older cohorts.

In terms of reporting frequency, which mirrors overall effectiveness of ethics and compliance programs, Millennials are more likely to report misconduct when they can (1) use company resources (such as a hotline), (2) feel prepared to handle an ethical dilemma (through effective training), (3) talk to an ethics advice resource in the company, and (4) rely on coworkers for support. In contrast, Boomers rely most heavily on "formal provision of standards and resources of an ethics and compliance program and [its] successful integration into their work arena as well as signs the company is doing the right thing," according to the report. In other words, older workers are more likely to consult more formal company channels for guidance, whereas the first choice of younger workers is likely to be their families. Traditionalists and Boomers are least likely to talk to their coworkers about it.

These differences are illustrated in deciding whom to consider telling about workplace misconduct, which varies considerably among generations. Millennials' choices are more extensive and significantly different from those of older cohorts. The youngest group prefers to tell friends–65%, family–65%, government resources–28%, religious leaders–22%, social networks–21%, legal counsel–20%, and traditional media–17%. Boomers' choices, like those of Traditionalists, are much more conservative: government–14%, religious leaders–9%, social networks–4%, legal counsel–9%, and traditional media–3%. The percentage who make their initial report outside the organization is strikingly different among the generations: Traditionalists–14%, Boomers–13%, Gen Xers–7%, Millennials–5%. But the trend reverses if an additional or second report is deemed necessary: Millennials–19%, Gen Xers–18%, Boomers–15%, Traditionalists–13%. The *IMA® Statement of Ethical Professional Practice* states, "Each member has a responsibility to keep information confidential except when disclosure is authorized or legally required."

The different resources each generation uses are a strong influence in the role the ethics and compliance program takes in an organization. Some of the objectives of the programs include raising employee awareness of:

- The ethical standards of the organization,
- Available resources for additional help,
- Confidential mechanisms to report misconduct, and
- Consequences for violating the code of conduct.

Observations contained in the ERC report include:

- The younger the worker, the more his or her perceptions about ethics will be influenced by social interaction;
- The older the employee, the more hierarchy, structure, and visible company commitment matter;
- Culture makes a difference for all generations, but, for younger workers, culture is the sum of their interactions with other individuals, much of which is with coworkers. Older workers get their cues about culture from the company's stated values, messages from the top, and their beliefs about the organization as a whole.

The report provides considerable motivation for senior executives to develop and maintain an ethics and compliance program in their organizations that will consider the attitudes and expectations of workers from all generations. Effective training programs should be the hallmark of a strong ethical culture.

Social Networking at Work Is a Major Risk with Large Costs

The Ethics Resource Center (ERC) has been conducting nationally representative surveys of ethical attitudes, knowledge, and beliefs in the U.S. workforce since 1994. Its latest comprehensive report, *2011 National Business Ethics Survey®* (NBES), included a series of questions about social networks and the people who use them. The intriguing findings on this subject led ERC to perform a follow-up survey in 2012 that focused on employees' social networking activities. The resulting report, *National Business Ethics Survey of Social Networkers* (NBES-SN), found that the emergence of social networking has serious implications for the workplace. ERC believes "social networking is affecting the way work gets done, reshaping ideas about transparency and confidentiality, and even altering attitudes about the type of conduct that is acceptable in the workplace."

The Securities & Exchange Commission (SEC) provided an indication of the importance of social networking to financial markets on April 2, 2013, when it announced that companies can use social media outlets such as Facebook and Twitter to report key market-moving information to the general public. These actions comply with Regulation Fair Disclosure (Regulation FD) as long as companies inform investors which social media outlets will be used.

According to the NBES-SN, "Social networking is now the norm, and a growing number of employees spend some of their workday connected to a social network." In 2011, three-quarters of American workers at all levels reported that they belonged to one or more social networks. The 2012 report notes that the proportion is higher today. Contrary to popular belief, young workers aren't the only ones using social networks. While the rate for 18- to 45-year-olds was 83%, participation by those in the 45- to 63-year-old group reached 67%. A November 2013 presentation by The Infographic Show reported that 67% of people use social networks when they are supposed to be working. Analysis of demographic factors in the NBES-SN, including gender, management level, intent to stay, education, union status, and compensation status (hourly or salaried), confirms that the population of social networkers closely mirrors the overall working population in the United States. The issue showing the greatest difference between a social networker and the U.S. workforce as a whole is tenure. Fewer social networkers have either short (less than one year) or long (11 years or more) tenure at their employer.

The top social networks that the largest percentages of employees use are Facebook (95%), Twitter (43%), Google+ (37%), LinkedIn (37%), Pinterest (23%), MySpace (21%), and a personal blog (14%).

Active Social Networkers (ASNs), which are employees who spend at least 30% of their workday connected to one or more social networks, represent 10% of the workforce. ASNs are younger: Workers younger than 30 make up only 26% of the total workforce but represent about 47% of ASNs. Workers older than 45 make up 43% of the total workforce but only 13% of ASNs.

ASNs include more members of middle management and first-line supervisors (71%) than the workforce as a whole. Again, employees who are more likely to be ASNs include males, workers in publicly traded companies, workers between the ages of 30 and 44, workers with some college or a technical degree, workers with three to five years' tenure, employees who intend to stay one to two years, employees who intend to stay three to five years, middle managers, first-line supervisors, members of unions, and salaried employees.

According to the NBES-SN report, "Nearly three out of four social networkers (72%) say they spend at least some time on their social networks during every workday, and almost three in 10 (28%) say such activity adds up to an hour or more of each day they spend at work." More than a quarter (27%) of ASNs check a social network about every hour. Well over half (61%) of all hourly employees—who should be paid only for time spent working—say that none of the time they spend on social networking is related to work.

In fact, survey participants report that very little of the workday spent online is work related. One-third (33%) of those who spend an hour or more of the workday on social networking say that none of the activity is related to work. Another 28% say just a small fraction

(10%) of their time online has something to do with their job. Just 14% confine their social network use to their lunch period or other unpaid time, meaning that employers are paying considerable sums for ostensible work time spent on personal matters. While many employees report only passive use of social networks to "connect" or "consume," more than half (55%) are "creators" who post commentary, write blog posts, or otherwise share their thoughts, including those about work-related issues.

This is particularly true of ASNs, who are unusually vulnerable to risks relating to ethical issues since far more of them consider many questionable disclosures to be more acceptable than do other social networkers: 60% of ASNs are likely to comment if their company is in the news, 53% mention work projects once per week or more, 42% believe it's okay to post about their job if the company isn't named, 36% mention clients once or more per week, 35% mention management once or more per week, and 34% mention coworkers once or more per week.

The propensity of ASNs to broadcast information otherwise considered confidential poses significant risks to all organizations. According to the NBES-SN, "Management must assume that anything that happens at work; any new policy, product, or problem; could become publicly known at almost any time."

That isn't to say that ASNs only represent a risk to an organization—they are also more likely to witness and report wrongdoing. In "Ethics and Social Media: Where Should You Draw The Line?" Patricia J. Harned, president of ERC, told Sharlyn Lauby that "You could also look at another set of our responses—particularly the high number of active social networkers who reported misconduct—and say that social networkers behaved appropriately." And when they report misconduct, they experience retaliation more frequently than their colleagues. The survey states, "A majority (56%) of ASNs who reported the misdeeds they witnessed experienced retaliation as a result, compared to fewer than one in five (18%) of other employee groups."

In addition to jeopardizing the reputation of the organization, improper use of social networking may provide temptations for sharing confidential information about new products or other projects that may enable others to profit illegally from trading inside information. This risk is especially relevant to accountants, who have access to a vast amount of financial and other data.

Social networking may also be altering the nature of reporting relationships at work. More than four out of 10 supervisors (42%) have some kind of an online connection, such as a friend or follower, who is someone they supervise. Among ASNs, the incidence of such

linkages rises to 60%. Supervisors who connect to social networks during the day are especially sensitive to how their posts will be viewed. "Among supervisors who spend 10% or more of their workday engaging in social networking, 84% say they consider what their direct reports will think when seeing the post," the survey notes.

To cope with the evolving importance of social networking in the workplace, the NBES-SN identifies several strategies for addressing these challenges. Organizations should:

- Develop broad-based strategies and social networking policies grounded in ethics and values, not merely compliance, so that employees are able to handle novel situations in an environment that continues to evolve. Only 32% of companies report having policies concerning social networking.

- Establish a social networking policy sooner rather than later, and reinforce it with training to reduce ethics risks for employees and management alike. It's important for rules to reflect today's realities of widespread use during the workday so that workers are more likely to abide by them.

- Take advantage of social networking to enhance internal and external communications, especially outreach to employees to reinforce the company's ethics culture.

- Invite social networkers to help shape social networking policy and to help the ethics/compliance function engage employees through social networking.

With social networking now the normal behavior for most employees, employers need to deal with the risks and opportunities it provides. The Infographic Show presentation reports that almost a third of companies either have no social networking policy or don't block access to certain sites. Employees should consider the consequences to themselves as well as their employer of every post they make. The continued growth of social media will only amplify these challenges in the future.